YOU PLAY TO
WIN THE GAME

YOU PLAY TO WIN THE GAME

LEADERSHIP LESSONS FOR SUCCESS ON AND OFF THE FIELD

NEW YORK JETS HEAD COACH
HERM EDWARDS

with SHELLEY SMITH

McGRAW-HILL

New York   Chicago   San Francisco   Lisbon
London   Madrid   Mexico City   Milan   New Delhi
San Juan   Seoul   Singapore   Sydney   Toronto

1 2 3 4 5 6 7 8 9 0 DOC/DOC 0 9 8 7 6 5 4

ISBN 0-07-144509-9

This publication is designed to provide accurate and authoritative information in regard to the subject matter covered. It is sold with the understanding that the publisher is not engaged in rendering legal, accounting, or other professional service. If legal advice or other expert assistance is required, the services of a competent professional person should be sought.

> —*From a declaration of principles jointly adopted by a committee of the American Bar Association and a committee of publishers.*

This book is printed on recycled, acid-free paper containing a minimum of 50 percent recycled, de-inked fiber.

McGraw-Hill books are available at special quantity discounts to use as premiums and sales promotions, or for use in corporate training programs. For more information, please write to the Director of Special Sales, Professional Publishing, McGraw-Hill, Two Penn Plaza, New York, NY 10121-2298. Or contact your local bookstore.

To my mother and father, for their endless sacrifices for me. Their love and words of encouragement have been a blessing in my life.

Contents

Contents

Contents

INTRODUCTION

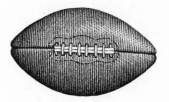

The wide gate and broad road leads us down the path of perception, which many people follow. The small gate and narrow road is reality, but only a few are willing to follow it.

–MATTHEW 7:13-14

For as long as I can remember, I've carried with me a black notebook in which I've collected what I call Life Lessons, sayings that reflect philosophies and beliefs that I refer to just about every day for guidance in my own personal life as well as in football.

I've formed most of them by listening to people I admire and respect, most of whom I know well. But I've also gotten them from a few people I don't know, but have learned from just the same. In each experience, I found wisdom and insight that hasn't necessarily caused me to succeed or fail at something, but has allowed me to analyze with great clarity why I succeeded or failed. These lessons have also gotten me through hard times. They've have become my blueprint for obtaining great peace and happiness in my life, both professionally and personally.

Many of these lessons were shaped by my experience as a kid growing up in Seaside, California, hearing, "It can't be done. You can't do that. That's never been done before." My answer, even early on, was, "Why not?"

My questioning was part curiosity and part rebelliousness. My father was a strict, disciplined military man who taught me the value of doing things the right way, but there was no questioning at home. It was "yes, sir" and "no, sir," and no gray area in between. But he also taught me that just because something has always been done a certain way doesn't mean it's right. Perhaps the biggest example came in his own personal life—my father was African American, and my mother is German. Fifty years ago, interracial marriages were not considered the "right" kind of marriage. But it was clear that my father asked, "Why not?" and found no reasonable answer.

Knowing that gave me a lot of strength when the desegregation program at my high school forced kids in Seaside to be bused to the predominantly all-white school across town. I didn't see it as a burden, even though I was on that bus for 20 minutes going to school and 20 minutes coming home. I saw it as an opportunity to meet different people and to play on a pretty decent football team.

Nobody thought I'd ever get out of Seaside. Nobody thought I'd play college ball or in the NFL, but I started 135 straight games, including Super Bowl XV for the Philadelphia Eagles against the Oakland Raiders. And nobody thought I'd be head coach of one of the greatest NFL franchises in history. But on January 18, 2001, I was announced as the new head coach of the New York Jets. Now they believe me.

I have never walked into anything thinking, "It can't be done." I've never been that way. It can be done if you believe it. And if you get enough people behind you who believe it, it becomes a great force that's hard to stop.

I've passed on many of my life lessons to my players as a way of helping them become better men. When I've been troubled or had to deal with some of the problems I've encountered in my life, I've gone back and read the lessons again and again, and through them, I've found a way to cope and grow. Now I pass the lessons on to you.

There are a lot of life skills that can be learned and taught through athletics. It's the same kind of pressure; it's the same approach. I've always thought that if I can make my players understand that there's really no difference in how you approach football and how you approach life, then they'll be okay on a lot of fronts. To me, it's all about getting through problems and knowing that you have the ability to get better—to do better—in everything you do. It's playing to win the game.

> To me, what Herman Edwards is about is special. And probably five things come to mind when I think of him. First is leadership, second is vision, third is conviction, fourth is a passionate pursuit of personal excellence, and fifth is that he's rarely, if ever, satisfied with things as they are. And there's a sixth that flows out of the fifth: He is a change agent.
>
> —*NFL Commissioner Paul Tagliabue*

Acknowledgments

All of my Life Lessons have been experienced at different phases in my life with a wide variety of people. To name everyone individually would be unfair—I may miss someone.

However, I do want to acknowledge that my Life Lessons were shaped by various family members, friends, teachers, and coaches. I am fortunate to be surrounded by good people who helped me to get where I am today.

To Shelley Smith—thanks for your assistance in putting my Life Lessons and experiences into words so that others can benefit.

Training Camp— Getting Ready to Succeed

Courage and initiative come when you understand your purpose in life.

–John C. Maxwell

For me, training camp begins the first day our season is over. Some seasons that's very early in January, but that doesn't matter to me. What matters is starting right then and there to work on our goals, correct our problems, and get us ready for what's next. In life, it means getting yourself ready for what you want to do to find the success you're looking for. Use the time wisely, because preparation is the biggest thing you can control on your way to where you want to be.

Find and Focus

Identify your goal and then create a plan. You've got to have a plan. If you don't have a plan, then you don't know which way to go.

When our season ends, the first thing I do is make a plan for the next one. I set my calendar, my schedule; I get the dates set from January to July so that everyone knows exactly what we're doing. I say, "Here's the dates; here's the plan. Here's where I want to go. January to July—bang—that's when training camp starts."

Now I can focus. I've got a start and a finish. Unless you understand where you're starting from and where you want to go, you can't get started. That's the hardest thing to do.

Remember when you got your first car? The first thing you did was look out the window every five minutes to make sure it was still there. You were sitting around with nowhere to go, hoping someone would call you to come over. You wanted to drive that car, so you would ask, "Mom, do you need something at the store?" You wanted to get in that car and go somewhere—you just needed a place to go.

It's the same thing when you're trying to accomplish something. There's a starting point. So now, where's the finishing point? You can't just start. You have to know where you're finishing, what's the end result. So you ask yourself, "Where am I trying to go?" "Well," you say, "I'm trying to go here—here's the start and here's the finish, here's where I want to go."

Once you have those, you're ready to draw the lines—the path you want to take to get from A to B, your plan for how you're going to get there. So you start making your plan, drawing the lines. But you don't draw them straight, because you're never going straight. That's not real life. You've got to allow for U-turns, reverses, left turns, right turns, ruts, speed bumps—all kinds of things that will present themselves as you go from A to B.

For example, say you're running a marathon. You know you've got a start, and you're pretty sure where the finish line is. But you don't run a straight line to the finish. You might move to the side, grab some water, find a different group of people to run alongside, but you feel that finish line pulling you. You know where you're going, and it's drawing you closer.

It's the same thing with a goal. Say you want to lose 20 pounds and you give yourself six months to do it. Okay, that's a reasonable goal. You set a start date, you set an end date, and you map out what you're going to eat, when you're going to exercise, and how long you're going to exercise. You allow for a few U-turns, a few chocolate chip cookies or something, because you know you can't just eat salad for six months. But that's okay; you planned for it, so when it happens, it doesn't derail the whole thing. By the finish date, you've got the work done.

The day training camp starts in July, I know we've accomplished what we needed to do to start the next step. We've found our focus and the first part of our plan. Now we're ready to do it again. I tell my guys that having the ability to precisely define our goals and create a plan to achieve them shapes our entire attitude and the way we view life.

Create Visions, Not Dreams

To me, dreaming is when you fall asleep and you dream and you're having all these thoughts, and then you wake up and go on to something else. You still had that dream; you just didn't act on it. A vision is a dream with a plan.

For example, say you're dreaming of becoming a concert pianist. You think about it all the time, imagining yourself on the stage playing in front of thousands of adoring fans. You dream and dream, but you never take a piano class. When you have a vision, you first dream of becoming a great pianist, then you find out where and when the piano classes are held, how much they are going to cost, how you're going to get the money to pay for the lessons, and how you're going to get to the classes, and then you sign up and show up for class. It's saying, "This is what I want to accomplish," and then asking, "Okay, how do I go about doing it?" It's creating an understanding about where you want to go and how to get there and not letting circumstances alter that goal.

You can visualize all you want about what you want to accomplish, but unless you put that visualization into action, all you have is an image.

When I was young, if someone had told me I would become head coach of the New York Jets, I would have looked at him like, "You've got to be kidding me." I didn't know exactly what my vision was way back then, but looking back now, I can see that I eventually created a vision of being who I am today.

Early on I knew I wanted to be a professional football player, if not a professional football coach. Because of that, I put a plan in place. I had help from a lot of coaches I seemed always to be surrounded by. My father was a serviceman, so he wasn't home all the time. My mom worked, too, to help support our family. So basically I grew up around coaches. They taught me a lot of life skills through athletics—trust, being on time, how to work with different people. Many of those lessons cross over from sports to real life. I learned that it didn't matter if one guy liked this kind of music and that guy liked a different kind of music, or if this guy was driving one kind of car and the other guy didn't have a car at all. When you come together for a common cause—like winning a football game, for example—all the little differences among you get thrown out. You are brought together and bound by a goal: to play the game as it should be played on the biggest stage with the highest of expectations. Somewhere down the line, that became my long-term vision, and everything I've done since has been about figuring out what it is that I need to do to get there.

I knew that it would take a lot of hard work, which is something I've never backed away from. I also knew that I needed to learn as much as I could about playing football, and so I devoured anything I could find about the game. I watched football; I talked football; I lived and breathed football. I questioned my coaches about everything they were teaching me, which at times got me in trouble. In fact, I asked so many questions that many of them began to consider me something of a rebel.

You have to remember that I was a teenager in the 1960s. And even though students all across the country were questioning everything from Nixon and the Vietnam War to drugs and music, it wasn't happening in football. Several of my coaches were stuck in the 1950s, in the "Yes, sir; no, sir," era, in which nobody, and I mean nobody, questioned why the coach told you to do something. Nobody except me. I have always wanted to know why I was being asked to run a certain drill or perform a certain task. It's not that I was obstinate, it was that I was curious and wanted to know everything I could about what I was being asked to do.

That didn't sit well with a lot of the guys who were coaching me. But I certainly didn't let their views alter my vision. I realized that their opinion of me became an obstacle only if I let it become one. Most people thought I'd never get out of Seaside, never make it to college, never play pro ball, and never coach. Had I dwelled on what they thought and let their judgment eat at my psyche, I might have proved them right.

Instead, I focused on my vision and refused to let anything get in the way. I talk to my players all the time about not letting circumstances or obstacles threaten our vision. I tell them, "Let me handle that part; you just focus on what we're trying to do."

I realized, on my way to becoming the head coach of the Jets, that sometimes pursuing the vision means breaking down the vision. In the 2002 and 2003 seasons, that meant breaking it down so far that the vision amounted to simply winning a game. Just one game. I gathered my team together at crucial points in both of those seasons and told them to focus simply on getting one win. "Just win the next game. That's all you've got to think about. Just win the next game."

I told them to let me worry about all the hits we were taking from the media and the fans and, oddly, even our own guys. Both seasons it came down to, "You guys just do your job. Concern yourself with the details of our vision to win the next game and how to get us there. Find out what it is that you need to do and do it. That's it. Nothing else."

And once I broke it down to the simplest of terms, my point finally got across, and we were able to get back on track. We finished both seasons strong and with the pride that we had not let circumstances push us completely off the path that would lead us to our goals.

It's like a student who is going to college to become a teacher and something happens at home with his family. Well, he can still become a teacher. He doesn't have to let his family situation keep him from achieving what he's set out to achieve. Circumstances may alter the path a bit, but you can't let them turn you back around. All the time we see people using a negative situation to justify why they didn't become what they set out to become. They see the situation as a way out of pursuing their goals, rather than something they need to push through to accomplish those goals.

You can't start running for the fire exit when there's no fire. You have to keep to your vision, stick with your plan. Dealing with hardships and obstacles is part of the process of obtaining success. It's a necessary part of learning. If you can find the strength to battle through and stay the course, you are bound to reach the pinnacle that you are aiming for.

I created my vision early in my life, and I've now been in professional football for 25 years. I didn't do it by myself, certainly, but I did do it by staying focused and by weathering the things that threatened to derail my plan. It's an important concept that I try to give to all the children I meet in the various camps I help organize and even children I just meet through daily life. Dreaming is great, but dreaming with a plan and a vision can make that dream come true.

Put Everybody in a Position to Succeed

As a coach, you always have to discover what it is that your players can do and what they cannot do. All of them have something you can't fix. Sometimes it's slow feet. Sometimes it's awkward lateral movement. Sometimes it's as simple as arm strength or leg strength. You take each player's limitation and you massage it, you hide it, you create another way to do it, but you don't do it in a way that exposes his weakness. You find another way that allows him to succeed.

It's like this: If you give a guy who has no arms a glass of water, you're not doing him any good. He's real thirsty, but there is no way for that guy to drink that glass of water. How are you going to get him that water? Give him a straw. Now he can drink the water.

Suppose someone you know is afraid of heights and the only way to get to the other side, where you've got to go, is to walk across a bridge suspended high above a canyon. "You're afraid of heights?" you ask. "Okay, then," you say, "close your eyes. You don't have to look. Close your eyes, give me your hand, let's go." You find a way for him to cross that bridge.

Now, that doesn't mean it always works. Maybe that guy needs to cross a bridge and you're not around. Maybe he needs to drink that water and there are no straws. Then what? What you do then is give him options, a safety net. You devise a plan for what he can do when he finds himself in a situation where he knows he doesn't usually find a lot of success, and you find him a way to get across that bridge.

The example I think of most is what happens when you get on an airplane. You get on and sit down, and the flight attendant walks down the aisle before you take off and tells you that if something happens, here's the mask, here's the oxygen. She's telling you that if something bad happens, this is what you do. She's saying, now, we don't want anything to happen. The pilot shouldn't screw this up, but if he screws it up, here's the mask, here's the lifejacket, here's the door, and here's how you kick it open. She's given you a plan so that you don't panic if something happens.

With players, it's the same thing. The last thing you want them to do in a situation on the field is panic. With panic comes chaos, and chaos leads to more chaos. So you talk about all the bad things that could happen: The wide receiver zigs in when you were expecting out and you aren't the fastest guy on the planet; they call a blitz when you weren't expecting it and you've got slow feet. Well, here's what you do: You play the angles and cut off that receiver, and when you see the blitz, well, son, you'd better get rid of that ball. You put a player in a position to succeed, even when the situation threatens to expose his weakness.

When I was coaching John Lynch in Tampa, I knew what he could do very, very well. And I knew what he couldn't do well, which I'm not going to reveal here because John Lynch is one of my best friends and the godfather to our son, Marcus. I'd hate for some coach to pick up this book and suddenly John's out of the league. But early on, I said to John,

"Here's what you do good. And that's what I want you to do every time. But if you find yourself in a situation where this over here happens, I want you to do this."

When we changed quarterbacks during the 2002 season in New York, I knew I had to give the new guy all the help I could. Vinny Testaverde had been struggling, and I decided that our backup, Chad Pennington, was going to have to take over. Here's a young guy getting his first start on a team that commands about the most media coverage in the entire country. He's a kid who came from a tiny school in West Virginia (Marshall),where he made some big-time passes to Randy Moss and made a name for himself, and he's suddenly being called on to play savior to our team, which at the time happened to be 1–3. I couldn't have Chad panic. I couldn't have his weaknesses exposed. Not in the first game, not when the expectations were so high. I believed in Chad's abilities, and I believed he was ready to meet the challenge. But I also believed that the kid could perceive this as being fed to the lions.

Vinny Testaverde handled his demotion with the most class I've ever seen from someone in that situation. I know it had to be hard for him, but he never showed it. He had seen how Chad handled being the number two guy for two years, being nothing but supportive, and Vinny returned the favor, working with Chad all week long on everything from reading defenses to footwork.

I picked a home game on purpose for Chad's first start, figuring that the home crowd would be behind him and the opponent off guard because it had seen him for only a few downs the season before, and yet because of that, he had a certain familiarity with who he was facing.

We lost the game in the final minute, but I was heartened because we were still in it at that final minute. Even though we lost, I told the team, "We're OK. We competed for 50 minutes." That's all I wanted. In my mind, Chad had succeeded. His confidence wasn't shot because he had us in the game until the very last minute.

If you're a history teacher and your students hate the idea of having to learn about events that happened long before their time, find a way to make it a game or set up a contest to see who can contribute the most or figure out the puzzle first. There's competitiveness in all of us. If you're in charge of employees who are habitually late, find a way to reward those who make it on time—even though that's already a part of the job requirement.

What this means is, you assess a situation, find out what people's strengths and weaknesses are, and then develop a plan that invites them to either correct the weakness or fuel the strength.

I've always thought the penalties for drunk driving were good and harsh, which they should be. When I did some research and found out how many repeat offenders there are, I began thinking we need to step up those penalties a little. But then I heard about a program that rewards people for staying sober behind the wheel. The Anaheim Angels give their fans free admission, free food, and free sodas if they agree to sign a form saying that they will be a designated driver. It's been very successful, and the number of DUI convictions after games in Anaheim has gone down dramatically. People like to feel good; they like to be rewarded. Play to that strength and make them the good guys in addition to tearing down the bad guys. Drunk driving is nothing to mess with, but successful solutions come in many different packages.

I believe there is always something you can do to make the situation success-friendly. Your son is failing math—find one of his classmates and ask him to tutor your son after school for a few dollars. Your wife is worn down and cranky because she's under the gun at work and can't even get a break to go for lunch—take lunch to her or make it for her in the morning before you go to work. You can't make it through a day on your diet—throw out the junk food. A little action can create the environment for a better result. Your son passes math. Your wife comes home happy, and you lose a few pounds. You put everybody in position to succeed.

Create Inconvenience

When you get comfortable, that's when you make mistakes. You find that sleepy place where you're not ready to move, you're not as hungry to achieve, and then you've forgotten what it was that brought you to where you are. Every now and then, you've got to change the way you do things to get the best out of the people you are trying to lead—even yourself. People get into a comfort zone where things are repetitive and dull, and you find that nobody is getting any better because everything has become rote, by memorization. It's like a food line worker in a canning factory. Every day he's there punching cans, punching cans. That's all he does every day. He never becomes better at anything else because he's doing the same job over and over. Mentally, he'll never get any better.

That's why I'll mix up practice sometimes. Maybe it's 5 below zero and everybody automatically starts walking over to the indoor practice field because that's what we usually do when it's that cold. So they'll head to the field without even checking to see if that's the plan. That's when I'll yell out, "Okay, boys, outside," and we go out to practice in that bitter cold. It gets their attention quickly, I'll tell you that. It makes them think, and it keeps them sharp. Creating inconvenience shakes things up—physically and mentally.

It also prepares my guys to perform in any kind of situation. This was never more true than when we were getting ready to play a game in New York just 12 days after the terrorist attacks. Now, I'm not saying we had gone through anything like that in advance, so that we were prepared. Not in the least. In fact, we had attempted to practice the day after the attacks, but I could see that our players and our staff were really hurting. We had people who live down the street from us who hadn't come home yet. It was a really tough deal for all of us, and football was the farthest thing from our minds. So I called off practice. But here we were 12 days later and still hurting, but the game was right in front of us and we were going to have to go and play even though nobody's heart was really in it.

I talked to my guys about what it was going to be like out there. I told them it was not an ideal environment or atmosphere in which to play a football game, but we all have to do hard things in life. I used the New York rescue workers, who were still sifting through huge piles of destruction, as an example. That certainly wasn't an easy job for them, but it was necessary because that's what rescue workers do. We're a football team, and playing football is what we do. I had to get them to understand that the day was going to be extremely emotional—both for us and for our fans—but that we were going to have to go compete and not give up because a lot of people were counting on us to play hard and, perhaps, create a small diversion from the tragedy we had all just been through. And then I reminded them how we had practiced and practiced well in nonideal environments.

We had come together as a team and made it through those subzero practices, and we did well. We had somehow found the energy to make it through that, and we were going to do our best to find the energy to make it through this.

As a player, I had never been through anything as tough as that game. But I did know a little bit about finding a good performance despite the conditions or atmosphere. When I was with the Eagles in the late 1970s, every fall we were forced out of Veterans Stadium by the Phillies and had to practice at John F. Kennedy Stadium, which made the Vet look like a palace. We'd dress at the Vet and drive our cars, in our uniforms, to JFK. There was a track around the field, and guys would race around it like they were in the Indy 500 until our coach, Dick Vermeil, found out and put a stop to it. But I think practicing in that crummy field and in situations we weren't accustomed to made us tougher and paid off when we had to play in adverse conditions later in the season.

With the Jets in 2002, one of our bigger inconveniences or wakeup calls was when I decided to make a change at quarterback. The quarterback taking over, Chad Pennington, had been with the Jets for two seasons but had gotten only a few reps in a couple of games. But we were in trouble, and I knew I needed to shake things up good. I could have changed the left guard or changed the safety, but I knew the team would simply say, "Okay, so what? He changed the left guard, and he changed the safety." But when you change the quarterback, then you're sending a message with shock waves attached, and now they're saying, "Man, if he changes the quarterback, he could very well change me."

I made sure they knew that this was not an act of desperation, that I wasn't suddenly panicking, because I had told them I wouldn't ever do that. I simply said I thought it was time to see what Chad could do. And I told them that it wasn't a change for just one game, that this was his team now, and his job was to win games. It was amazing to watch the effort level rise almost immediately. They knew I wasn't playing, and they also knew that they needed to give Chad their best effort so that he—and the team—could succeed. It gave my players the jolt they needed, and we found ourselves a pretty good quarterback in the process.

You find out a lot about the people you're leading when you throw something new and difficult at them. Do they respond and step up, or do they look at you like you're the crazy man who just messed things up? But I believe you've got to change something when staying the same isn't getting it done. I'm not a guy who's going to holler and shout and belittle people, and I'm not changing that. But I am going to make changes, swift changes, and I don't blink when I do it.

Delegate Leadership

When you are in a leadership position, you're generally not trying to lead just one person. It's easy to lead one person. But how do I get 53 people to understand my vision? Not everybody's going to agree. Not everybody is going to think that what I want him to do is good for him.

So I find my guys—the guys I invite up to the house, who sit with my wife and me and their wife—and I tell them what I want this team to be about. We do it one at a time. It's January, our season's over, but I've got the quarterback and his wife over for dinner. The Super Bowl hasn't even been played yet, but I'm getting ready for what we're going to try to do next season. And that means the quarterback needs to come up to the house, and we need to talk. And then I'll do it with the next guy. I'll probably do it with about 10 guys, and I do this so that when we walk into mini-camp in March, they, in turn, tell their guys, "I know what the coach wants. This is what we're doing; let's go."

By taking a player out of the workplace, I'm giving him a platform so that he can lead, too. Sitting around the dinner table, we don't talk so much about work as about philosophies. In business and in football, there are cliques. You pick the leaders of those groups and make them understand why you're doing something, because a lot of times, when you're the leader and you do certain things, people say, "Why is he doing that?" And when I've got 10 guys who know the answer, they can say to those people, "Here's why we're doing that; coach told me." They're explaining what my philosophy is in a more detailed fashion. You can't go out and do that with every single player on your team, so you pick your guys and you get them to spread the message.

Larry Bird was perhaps one of the best I've seen at delegating to find success. He got his first coaching job as the head guy with the Indiana Pacers. Larry's smart, but Larry hadn't coached before. But he knew what to do. He hired Dick Harter to run the defense and Rick Carlisle to run the offense, and then he sat back and watched. He was around the team, and he talked to the players about motivation and hard work, and that team was the best-conditioned team in the league. But when it came to running the offense and defense, he let his guys take charge. He hired experts to handle the details and oversaw the big picture.

To some extent, that's what we've done in New York. I hired good people, and I let them do what they do best. I can't be involved in every single position on this team. I can't do it all myself. It's impossible. I've seen guys who tried to do it all, and all they did was wear themselves out, because you can't be in all those places. It won't work. That's why, when I hear a guy saying that he wants to be the general manager and the head coach, it says to me that he has no family life because he never wants to go home. My hours just being the head coach are crazy enough. I'm at the office at 4:30 a.m. thinking, "How could anyone be a good GM and a good head coach? How do you do all that?"

What you do is hire people that you trust. People that when you ask them to do something, they'll do it. I've seen situations where all of a sudden a guy becomes a coordinator, and when the head coach tries to implement something, the coordinator's arguing, "No, but . . ." He's arguing with the head coach, and I'm saying, "Hey, that's the head coach. If he says we're running that play, you need to run that play. There's no discussion."

I made sure I hired the kind of guys who think like me. I told them, "Don't worry about what happens. If what I tell you to do doesn't work, I'll take the hit. You just keep coaching."

Day to day, I pop in and listen in on meetings, or during drills on the field, but I let my guys coach and teach, and I contribute when I can in the best way I can. I keep the pace moving; I keep the focus sharp and the players always guessing about what I'm going to do next. Don't hire good people and then micromanage them. Nothing sends an organization into chaos faster and with a fouler scent. Don't hire a secretary and then do the typing for him. Don't commission a tailor and then sew it for her. You've got to trust the people you hire and trust their abilities.

You've also got to make absolutely sure that the people you delegate understand exactly what you're trying to do and why. The tailor can't make the suit you want unless she knows what you want it for and why you want her to make it. The secretary can't type the report unless he knows what it is you want him to type.

My coaches can't coach unless they understand my plan. Every spring, the first thing we do is meet, and I hand them sheets of paper with my philosophy and expectations for the season:

> *My definition of a coach:* An expert in his field, he coaches with confidence and passion for the game of football. He develops his players and makes them meet the highest possible standards. He coaches his players to win.
>
> *My expectations:*
>
> *Be committed to excellence.* Every play, every practice, every meeting, every situation, every time.
>
> *Be positive.* Adopt a positive attitude. Players will respond better to a positive environment than to a negative one. Have energy.
>
> *Be prepared.* You cannot control which team wins a game, but you can determine how your players prepare to win.
>
> *Pay attention to details.* All aspects of a player's effort to prepare mentally, physically, and fundamentally are a coach's responsibility.
>
> *Be organized.* Make the best possible use of the available time and resources.
>
> *Be flexible.* You must have the ability to respond and adapt to change.

Be ethical. You must exhibit integrity in all of your
dealings with players and staff members. The
first thing you must do is have all the facts,
and then you can be constructive. If you are
constructive, you will be reflecting your
sincerity and dedication as well as your
personal and team integrity. If the facts
indicate that you made a poor decision or
that you took an improper action, then you
must admit that you were wrong. On the
other hand, if the evidence, based on those
facts, shows that you were correct, you must
stand firmly and fairly for what you believe
is right.

Emphasize sportsmanship. The game of professional
football must be coached and played in ways
that sportsmanship and a team's ability to win
a championship are never compromised.

Once my coaches know my philosophy and what I
expect, they can apply their knowledge to their specific
assignment. The wide receivers' coach can now teach the
wide receivers. The linebackers' coach can now teach the
linebackers. I trust their expertise as long as they follow my
plan.

And it's great because when I walk into the room, or
when I'm sitting in the back, I can hear them echoing what
I've told them. Everyone now knows what the program is,
and it's a good feeling. I feel good about my message, and
they feel good because they have a voice and they are allowed
to do their jobs.

The media got on Paul Hackett, our offensive coordinator, a little in the beginning of the 2002 season because the offense wasn't as productive as we would have liked. Half of it was because of me. I was telling Paul that we didn't need to pass the ball right now because we weren't good enough on defense to stop the run. I believed that we had no chance to win the game because we'd be on the field so long that the offense would never get the ball back. I told him that we had to control the clock, which means running the ball. Later, when our defense got better, we opened it up a little, and we ended up winning 10 games. So I guess we were doing something right. I delegated, but I oversaw, too.

This is an application that works in business just as easily as it does in football. Take out the words *player* and *coach* and insert *employee* and *employer*. It's a simple plan that's designed for success. But you don't have to take my word for it; how about that of Southwest Airlines? Here is what Southwest Airlines insists on:

> "We are committed to provide our Employees a stable work environment with equal opportunity for learning and personal growth. Creativity and innovation are encouraged for improving the effectiveness of Southwest Airlines. Above all, Employees will be provided the same concern, respect, and caring attitude within the organization that they are expected to share externally with every Southwest Customer."

Southwest Airlines has proven that it can "win" by empowering its employees.

Make the Will Stronger
than the Skill

I am living proof that if you outwork everyone else, you can make up for what you might lack in talent. Everybody's got skill. I tell my team that all the time. But you've got to make your will stronger than that of any of those guys you're playing against.

I was ignored in the 1977 draft because a lot of the NFL scouts believed I was too slow to play in the league. The first spring at San Diego State, I ran a 4.6 40—which is like running a 2-hour mile, almost. The coaches thought there was something wrong with the watch, but I kept running 4.6s. My coach, Claude Gilbert, was resigned to the fact that "that kid can't run." I knew I was slow (well, it was tough for me to admit it) but I made up for my lack of speed by being smarter. I played the angles, and I was amazing at anticipating where the play was going, which meant that I could get myself there in time to make the play. One day in practice with the Eagles, I broke up seven passes in a row. I hollered back at Dick Vermeil and said, "Keep 'em coming, coach. I'll be here all night long." And I meant it.

With the Jets, our quarterback, Chad Pennington, knew early on that he wanted to be a quarterback, but he also knew that he wasn't the most mobile guy on the planet. He also knew that he didn't have Vinny Testaverde's arm or Michael Vick's legs, he told me, so he knew that he had to find other ways to get the job done. His father tells a story about Chad when he was a junior in high school in Knoxville, Tennessee, and how Chad got up at chapel service and told the congregation he knew how hard he would have to work if he was going to be good enough to play football in college. Nothing came easy for him.

The University of Tennessee asked him to walk on, but Chad chose to go to Marshall University instead and became a starter with a guy named Randy Moss on the receiving end. He did it by outworking everybody else on that roster, and that's how he came to be our starter, too.

Sitting back, waiting in the wings, he studied Testaverde's every move and asked infinite questions about the game: different coverages, different plays. He worked on the physical and mental sides of what it takes to be a successful quarterback. His father says that at Marshall, Chad took the most challenging classes with the most demanding professors and finished with a 3.8 GPA. I knew we were dealing with someone who met challenge prepared and head on.

Chad got his first start five games into his third season, and he quickly established himself as one of the premier young quarterbacks in the league. At one point that first season, he led the league in completion percentage and ranked second in passer ratings. The list read like this: Marc Bulger, St. Louis; Chad Pennington, NY Jets; Rich Gannon, Oakland; Brett Favre, Green Bay; Drew Bledsoe, Buffalo. Not bad company for a first-year guy.

He didn't do it by raw athletic ability. He willed it to happen.

I was once told a story about Antonio Stradivari, a seventeenth-century violin maker. He believed that to make a violin less than his best would be to rob God. He was right. God could not make Stradivarius violins without Antonio, and Antonio knew that he owed it to God and himself to be the best.

If what you want to become is worth pursuing, it is worth pursuing with all your heart and might. If you want to land that big promotion, arrive early and stay late. Do things that nobody else is doing. Go to things that your company says aren't required. Take an interest in other aspects of the company. Develop new skills while you hone the ones you already have. Ask questions. Find out what qualities seem to be the most important for that promotion. Talk to people. Collect business cards. Follow up with calls.

There are many business success stories out there about someone coming from nothing to become something great simply because he put in extra elbow grease every day. Jimmy Carter started out as a peanut farmer. Arte Moreno, who bought the California Angels a year ago, started out building billboards. Their skills didn't necessarily lend themselves to becoming successful in their respective businesses and then achieving their later goals. They simply wanted and worked toward their goals harder than anyone else.

I can teach you to tackle. I can teach you to run. But I can't teach you how hard to tackle or how fast to move your legs. I can read a book about love and relationships, but the book isn't going to be the one making the effort to do things better at home. It has to be inside you.

Make the Grass Your Blackboard

A person's real leadership is not seen while she's sitting behind a desk. I tell my assistants all the time, you can do all the classroom and film work you want, but it's getting down and dirty with the players, showing them exactly what you want them to do, that gets the job done.

Here's why: You put on some film of your next opponent playing some other team, and the tape starts going, and
my player sees some guy get hit in the mouth, and he starts
visualizing seeing stars and blood coming out of his nose,
and then all that film study goes out the window. All the
player is thinking is, "That guy is going to hit me in the
mouth." So now what do I do? I can't show him how to block
that guy on a film. I've got to get out there on that field and
show him, "This is what you've got to do."

Not everyone can take what he sees on a video or on a
blackboard and apply it on the grass. Actually, I'd say the
majority of our players fall into that category. Some guys are
more visually oriented than others. John Lynch was one of
the few who could see something once and then go out and
do it. But most guys can't do that. You've got to take them
out on the field and repeat what was on that video or on that
blackboard and do it over and over again. You've got to put
your feet in the dirt and say, "This is how you do it now."
You've got to find a way to teach everybody because everybody doesn't learn the same way. Plus, I find that my younger
players are impressed that I can still go out and do what it
is that I'm trying to get them to do.

I find the same thing with kids, too. At my camp, which
we have annually for more than 500 kids in Monterey, California, near where I was raised, I'm out there on the field all
the time, demonstrating moves, footwork, routes, and catch-
ing techniques. And it's what I tell the guys who volunteer
their time to help coach these kids, too. You can make them
sit down and read a playbook, but it's always more effective if
you show them yourself how to do something the right way.

It's a good technique, and not just in football. Say you
want your kids to learn good manners—show them by exam-

ple. If they see you doing things the right way, they naturally will follow. Correct them, of course, when they make a mistake, but don't become one of those "do as I say, not as I do" parents if you want your children to exhibit the right kind of behavior.

In business today, everyone seems to be obsessed with PowerPoint programs. They put up a big screen and take their employees through a step-by-step explanation of how to do something, like filling out time sheets or expense reports. They spend hours giving their employees information, showing them these slides, quizzing them on what the procedure is, and then when it comes time to actually fill out the form, most of the employees have already forgotten what they've been told. I think it would have been far more effective if the manager of the group had given the employees an actual form and allowed them to fill it out and make mistakes and ask questions and really get the process embedded in their minds. Doing always has a bigger impact than showing. If you want someone to learn a task, show him first. Don't just talk to him.

Understand that Life Is Not a Dress Rehearsal

You don't get life back. So it's up to you to make sure that you are trying to be the best at what you do at all times. Dress rehearsals are for Broadway productions and weddings. In life, God gives you a talent. It's up to you to figure out what it is, and once you do, you'd better use it to the best of your ability. Don't settle for being good. Aspire to be great.

I put my players in pads the first day of training camp every season so that they get used to them. Because it's generally ugly when you first put them on, whenever it is. They're like new shoes. They're nice shoes, they look good when you put them on, but they don't really fit your foot real good right away; you have to wear them for a while until they fit. It's the same thing with shoulder pads and helmets. Get them out of the way so you can concentrate on the real deal. Because each day we're going out there, and we're going to practice with a purpose and go out there and compete. We practice with a purpose every time we step onto the field—it's no dress rehearsal out there. Getting used to the pads is part of that reality and part of getting us prepared.

It's the same with preseason games. I don't count preseason games as preseason games. I want to win every one. They all count to me. I don't care if I'm playing marbles against the Pittsburgh Steelers, I want to win. Because that's a chance to compete to try to win. That's what life is about. It's about winning. Never forget that your job is about winning and being the best. Because before you know it, it's over, and you could be sitting there saying, "What if I had done this, what if I had done that." But now it's too late.

Take advantage of opportunities. They come about all the time, and the worst thing you can do is waste them. I personally have been given one of the greatest opportunities of my life in being head coach. It took a lot of guts to hire me. I owe this organization everything I've got, and I'm not wasting this opportunity.

First Quarter— Digging in

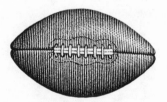

A man's wisdom gives him patience.

—Proverbs 19:11

Once you're ready, you feel prepared to put in that game plan, and then it's time for the kickoff and the first quarter. That's when you set the tone of the game. It's a feeling-out process where you figure out how best to implement all that preparation and development. The first quarter is always a little unstable because you don't know quite what's going to happen, even though you've done all this work to prepare. But you've got to have a first quarter to get to the second, so you set your parameters early, set the table for what you're getting ready to accomplish.

Teach the Why

To be an effective leader, you've got to teach people why you want them to do something and why it works. You can't just walk into a room and announce, "This is what we're doing, boys"—not if you want to accomplish something. You can say, "This is what we're doing, boys," but you need to add, "and this is why we're going to do it that way." When you do that, your chances of getting it done go up dramatically because now there's no room for them to say they didn't understand.

Growing up, I was always asking, "Why?" Somebody would say, "Do this," and I'd say, "Why?" It wasn't that I didn't believe in authority, it was just that I questioned it.

And that was something that back then an athlete never did. You were never supposed to question authority. If a coach said this, you did it, no questions. But I asked questions anyway because I wanted to know the answers.

A coach would say, "Do this footwork drill," and I'd look him straight in the eye and say, "How is that going to help me be a better football player?" He'd look at me crazy and say, "Son, what the heck are you talking about? You think you know everything?" I'd say, "No, I just want to know why we're doing that." Sometimes he'd tell me, more often he wouldn't, but I did what he said with or without an explanation—although I was a much more willing participant if I knew why I was doing something.

Back then coaching styles were a lot different from what they are now. But learning about why we were doing something allowed me to be part of it and to understand the process better. I knew that in order for me to do whatever it was they were asking as perfectly as I could, I had to know why. It made me a more effective part of the team.

I believe that when you want to accomplish something, you've got to give the people who can do it for you as many tools as possible to make it happen. It gives them understanding, and it also makes them feel like a more important part of the process. For example, a guy on an assembly line can be tightening bolts all day and know only that he's tightening bolts. But let that same guy know that the bolts he tightens are what keeps the engine from falling through the frame, which keeps the car from crashing, which keeps people safe, and I'm guessing he then has a better appreciation for what he's doing and will take greater care in his work.

Remember when you were a kid and your dad told you to go to bed by 8 o'clock and you asked, "Why?" and he said, "Because I said so." Well, okay, you should do what your dad says, but if he had answered, "Because you've had a long day today and you have a big day tomorrow where you're going to need all your strength," then it might have tempered your disappointment at having to go to bed at 8 o'clock and you might have marched right up to bed with no argument. That, of course, is simplifying things a little bit, but it's important to know that nobody responds well to, "Because I said so."

You can order people around all you like, but without an explanation, all you'll do is alienate people. Tell your assistant that you need the toxicology reports for that piece of property by Thursday, but also tell him that you need them by Thursday because the county inspector is coming by the office and she's been laying the heat on you about the levels. Now you've included your assistant in the project as part of your team instead of treating him as someone who merely works for you.

I try always to tell my players why we're doing certain drills, practicing shorter or longer, and why we work on certain things on certain days. I'm the head coach, yes, and I suppose I could just bark it out and they'd do it, but by letting them in on my thought process, I am including them in what we're trying to accomplish.

Before a game, I always spell out the game plan because they all want to know what's the game plan. "What's the game plan, coach?" they keep asking. I say, "Okay, men, here's the game plan. Here's the first part; here's what we're going to do. We're going to do it because we think it will work against what they're throwing at us. Here's the second part, here's the third part, and here's how we finish the job."

Once I do that, I know it's all in their heads. I've established parameters. I've told them what we're going to do and why and here's how. They can focus now on the project because we all know the game plan. No one's above the game plan.

Players may work for you, but that doesn't mean they're less important to the goal. Teach 'em why and they'll have a better understanding of what you're trying to do.

You Don't Have to Be a Bully

You don't have to be a bully to get things done. What you do have to be is consistent. Decide who you are and stick with it. I told my players with the Jets the very first day I met with them that I was not going to yell at them. I said I would not rant and rave. I told them I wasn't going to do that because it wasn't my style. "You never have to worry about me calling you out in public. I don't play games like that," I said. "If we've got an issue, you come see me. We'll talk. We'll get it figured out. But I will not yell and scream because to me, that's just wasting my voice."

I think 25 years ago, or maybe even 20 years ago, a coach might have had to use those screaming, berating tactics to get his players' attention. There are a few out there today who still believe that that works, and sometimes it does. But whenever I encountered those kinds of coaches when I was growing up, all it did was make me say, "I'll never coach like that." The last thing I want to do is be on television grabbing a player by the collar and hollering at him or running out on the field and hollering at the officials. Today, I believe you have to embrace your own personality and gauge the personality of your team. I know who I am. And so I'm not going to try to be something else.

Our best running back, one of the best in the league, Curtis Martin, told me that when he was a rookie with the New England Patriots, his coach, Bill Parcells, made him run the same play over and over again to see if Martin would break. That's Parcells's way. And it's a way that has made him one of the best football coaches in history. That's his way, but mine is different. That doesn't mean one is right and one is wrong, despite his record. It's just that his way worked for him. I think, so far, that my way works for me. I know Curtis Martin's will, and I know that he will never break. So I know that I don't need to test him. Maybe Parcells didn't know that when Curtis was a rookie, but I'll bet he knows that about him now. Curtis Martin will never break. If a coach tells him to do something, he's going to do it. I have unbelievable confidence in him. I don't need to try to break him down.

And another thing I've learned along the way: When you holler at the top of your lungs at people, all you really get is a bad headache. I'm certainly not going to holler at a guy in the middle of a game. First of all, nobody hears you anyway. The players aren't listening; they're watching the game. It maybe looks good for TV because the announcers say, "Look at the coach; he's going crazy, he's so involved in the game."

But the fact is that the calmer I can be, the more the team is calm, especially when things are going badly. When a player makes a mistake, I don't really need to go jump in the guy's face. He already feels bad. I'll walk over and talk to the guy, but I don't make a big deal out of it. I generally don't do it right after the play, either, because the guy is still upset about the mistake to begin with. I pick and choose when I'm going to go and get the guy, and I speak to him in a teaching voice, where I'm trying to figure out what he was thinking. I listen, and then I tell him, "Okay, here's what we need to do." That's how I communicate with players in the heat of the battle.

Yelling and screaming at someone, whether it is in football, in business, or in your own home, only draws attention to yourself, and what does that accomplish? When your coworker makes a mistake, does yelling at her really make things better? Think about it. Wouldn't an even-toned query as to what she was thinking at the time seem a lot less confrontational? Confrontation only begets bad feelings, and I've rarely seen good things accomplished when bad feelings exist between people.

When someone makes a mistake, whether it be your coworker, your boss, or your kids, most likely that person already feels bad about what he did wrong. Screaming at him makes it worse, not better. Ask yourself, what is the goal? Isn't the goal to correct the mistake so it doesn't happen again and then move on? Hollering may sometimes be an effective tool. Sometimes you have to get mad and raise your voice to get your point across, but more often than not, I find that a soft voice and piercing eyes are just as effective, if not more so. The people you manage want to be respected and guided in the right direction that will earn them your praise.

Children, especially, need a map to follow. But parents need to understand that in enforcing the map, they must be consistent. If you start out by saying that you'll understand no matter what the problem is, make sure you are understanding when your son confides in you. Don't say you'll understand and then blow up when he comes home and tells you about a mistake he made. Don't throw his trust aside by losing focus because you're so disappointed. You told him you'd work through it with him. Try not to focus on the actual mistake, but rather on how he reacts to it—how he can learn and grow. That's what's important.

Now, that doesn't mean you shouldn't tighten the screws from time to time. But learn how to do it without standing on a soapbox letting everybody else know that you're tightening the screws. When one of my players gets into trouble, I read him the riot act, but I do it in private. I don't believe in airing dirty laundry in public. Don't tighten the screws with your son with his friends around, just as I don't do it with the rest of my team around. You don't need to hang people publicly to make them accountable. Do it behind closed doors; they'll get your point.

I think my team understands where I'm coming from. I've been consistent from the very beginning. The guys told me that after our very first game together back in 2001, which we lost, they were concerned about how I was going to react. But when I didn't come into the locker room ranting and raving and then didn't change practice, didn't make them run, didn't do anything differently, and didn't change my voice, that's when they knew we would be okay. I think if I had started yelling and screaming and changing the way we'd been doing things, then I would have lost them. Anything we accomplished after that would have come from emotion rather than achievement. Because I didn't panic, because I stayed consistent in both my demeanor and my beliefs on how things should be run, my players were able to say, "Coach is okay. And if he's okay, we're okay."

And I stayed the same way, even after our fourth straight loss in a row during the 2002 season. Flying home after that game in Jacksonville, I was worried about what I would tell the team and how I could convince them that changing the quarterback didn't mean that I was panicking. It was time to make a move. It wasn't out of desperation; it was because

Chad Pennington, I felt, was ready. But how could I convince my players that I wasn't desperate?

I stayed up much of the night coming up with a plan of attack so that when the players came back into work, they weren't just sitting around with their heads in the dirt, moaning, "What are we going to do?"

I didn't scream. I didn't holler. I didn't rant and rave. I told them we were changing the quarterback, and I told them in the same voice I'd used for two seasons. I let them know that I was concerned and that this was me trying to find a way out of our situation. I was myself.

Some people call me a players' coach. That's fine. That doesn't mean I'm soft. Dick Vermeil told me that means that I know how to communicate.

I know this: If I go down, I'll go down as I am. In my heart, I'm doing what I think is right every single day. That's all anyone can do.

Identify the Necessary Sacrifice

You find out a lot about a person when you ask, "What are you willing to give up to better yourself?" When I was growing up, over and over again I had to make the choice to either go work out or go hang out. And always, I chose working out, even though I was often ridiculed by my buddies, who said, "Oh, man, why didn't you go? You don't need to practice that much, man. You're just wasting your time." I told them I was willing to give up partying to get to where I wanted to go. And that was to become a professional football player.

I knew from the time I was eight years old that that was what I was going to do. I watched whatever team was playing on Sunday, and I said, "That's it. I'm going to play football on TV." Nobody believed me, of course, but I knew what I was going to do. "I am getting on that TV," I told my buddies. "That's what I'm going to be. I'm going to be a professional football player."

Looking back, I realize how lucky I was to have found something I was passionate about at such an early age. For some people, it takes an entire lifetime. But as an 8-year-old, I figured out my life's work. To a lot of people it sounded stupid. But I said, "Don't worry. I'm going to college, I'm getting a scholarship, and I'm going to play pro football." And then I set about preparing myself to do that.

I knew that to get there, I had to sacrifice the parties and the wild life that was trying to lure us all. This was the 1960s, remember, a time when a lot of kids my age were experimenting with drugs and alcohol and a lot of wild ideas about what was right and what was wrong. We had some heady things to think about: The Vietnam War was escalating, Martin Luther King was assassinated, and we put a man on the moon. A lot of kids were questioning a lot of things, and many rebelled against the system. To many, drugs and alcohol were a way of processing it all, or just a way to ignore it all.

To me, well, I didn't think an athlete should drink or smoke, and because I was going to be a professional athlete, I didn't. And I was ridiculed routinely. I'd get, "Oh, are you a narc? You working for the school?"

I was shunned by a lot of people who couldn't understand what I was trying to do. At times it was rough. Peer pressure at that age is intense, no matter what it is you're fighting.

"I'm getting on that TV," I told them. "I'm going to be a pro football player."

I knew that was what I was doing. And I also knew that whatever I had to do to prepare myself, I was willing to do it. And I knew I had to do it right then, during those years. If I wasn't good enough to make it, it wasn't going to be because I didn't work hard enough to prepare myself. I wasn't going to have that excuse. I've heard that excuse way too much from guys who were pretty good athletes but didn't go on; they got into trouble—jail, drugs, drink, all the vices got to them. Some of them were better than me athletically, but they weren't strong enough mentally.

Later, after I'd gotten where I said I was going, they all said, "Well, you were lucky." I wasn't lucky. I wasn't lucky to graduate from high school and get a scholarship to Cal and make it as an undrafted free agent. It wasn't luck. It was everything I gave up that other guys wouldn't. They couldn't see it back then; when they were going to Fifth Avenue, I had already made a turn and I was gone. Now, I wasn't perfect and I got close to that edge sometimes, but I always knew when I was getting too close to that edge, and I'd say, "I got to go." That, to me, was a blessing. The only luck I had was that I found out what I wanted to do in life early.

There's always something that needs to go for a person to find success. You want to lose weight? Give up chocolate, or that extra hour of sleep to go to the gym or take a walk. If it's something that's really worth succeeding at, you'll find out what it is that will keep you from reaching that goal. In business, it might be taking a year off to go back to school. You don't want to lose that year of income, give up that way of life, but you know you need that MBA if you're ever going to be running that company. So you scale back, you give up the extras—the meals out on the town, the pay-per-view movies, or that trip you always take during the summer—and you go to school.

Identifying what you have to sacrifice isn't always that clear. Sometimes you think you've already sacrificed so much and still that goal seems far off. That's when you go back over what you've been doing, what you've given up and what you haven't, and make adjustments. Sometimes the sacrifice doesn't seem right or fair. Working at a job far away from your family certainly fits into that category. But when you've spent three months looking for work around home and the only opportunity that presents itself is 3000 miles away, you take it so that you can continue to feed and support your family. It's a sacrifice, yes, but it's one that you should take pride in because you found success in what your goal was, taking care of things financially at home, and hopefully the person you're married to and your kids understand why you're doing it. If they don't, then you've got to talk to them and make them understand.

It was tough when I got the Jets job because it meant that Lia and I had to leave Tampa, Florida, where we had spent the last few years watching our son, Marcus, play football. It had been great to zip over to the high school when he had a home game to see him play. But I knew I'd have to sacrifice watching his games in order to reach my goal of becoming a head coach in the NFL. Lia knew it, Marcus knew it, and while none of us really liked the sacrifice, we all understood it was what I had to do, for all of us.

Real success never comes without some kind of sacrifice. The challenge is to identify it and act.

Watch the Clock

When you are late, you've just told me something. You've just told me and everyone else involved that you believe you are more important than we are. When a guy's late for a meeting or a practice, he gets fined. When he's late a second time, he doesn't start. If it gets to a third, he's out of a job. This is nonnegotiable. I've told my players, "I don't care how talented you are, how necessary to the team's success you are; if you're late, you won't be here anymore." I told them that I would not rant and rave about it. "I won't stand at the front of the meeting or at practice and scream and yell when you're late. But if you're late, you are not going to be here." There are guys who are no longer Jets because they didn't take me seriously.

Me? I'm always looking at the clock. My dad used to say that late is being five minutes early, so late was never an option for me, nor is it now.

Respect the Journey

If you focus on the process—how to get it done—rather than on the result, you always win. Winning matters, I won't lie, but you can't predict whether you're going to win or not. What you can do, though, is respect the road you must travel that is most likely to get you that win. In football, that means practicing hard every day, enjoying the effort you expend and the way your body feels at the end of the day, and taking care of yourself off the field, too, making sure that you get enough sleep, that you're eating right, getting yourself mentally set. I tell my players all the time that if they think about doing all those things to their best ability every single day, then on game day the rest will take care of itself. It puts the pressure on the preparation instead of the end result. I know that on Sunday, either we're ready or we're not.

It's something I learned from Tony Dungy when we were in Tampa. He and I are both old school. We have the same philosophy and believe that the same things are important. We both believe in fundamental football and winning in a simple kind of way. We both believe in how you do things rather than what happens because good things will come if you do things right.

If you think about it, you can't have success without the journey, without the process of getting to that successful point. That's why it's so important to make that journey your focal point.

Say you set a goal of losing 20 pounds. Okay, that's good. What's your plan? Well, you say, I'm going to exercise every day for an hour, cut out cakes and cookies, and eat salads and fish. Okay, that's your plan. You're ready to go. So day one comes and goes and you're stepping on the scale, and you don't see any difference. Day two comes and goes, and the same thing. Well, now you're frustrated; you're ready to give up and say it's no use. That's because you're focusing on the scale, not on the daily plan. Keep your thoughts on eating right and exercising right, and I guarantee that if you follow through, that weight will come off at some point. It might not be as quick as you want it to be, but if you respect the "how to get it done," then eventually you'll hit that goal.

Or say you're writing a big report. A huge report. It's supposed to be hundreds of pages long, and you have a deadline. You're gripping, you're panicked because how are you possibly going to write hundreds of pages in that amount of time? You spend more time worrying about that deadline than if you just sat down and wrote, say, 10 pages every day. If you keep doing that every day, sitting at the computer and writing those 10 pages, you will have that project done before you know it. You know you can't wait until the last minute, because it would be impossible to get it done. You set a plan, you formulate a process, and you keep yourself on schedule.

There have been many times during a season when I, myself, have had to keep myself focused on what we were doing every single day, rather than jump ahead to Sunday. Sometimes that's meant going back to fundamentals: working on footwork, lateral moves, special teams. But every day I commit myself to that process because I know that if we do everything right, we'll find a way to win that game Sunday. Of course it hasn't always worked. But that doesn't mean you throw out the process. You tweak it, you add a few things, you change this here and there, but you keep at it, every day, to the best of your ability mentally and physically. That way, even if you lose the game, you've gained knowledge and self-satisfaction.

Create Opportunity

Just as you must establish the run to create the opportunity to pass the ball in football, you've got to take action to open the door for possibility in business and in life. Because it's not just going to fall in your lap. You can't sit at home and wait for the phone to ring. And emailing somebody isn't going to cut it, either. I think email is the great antisocial crutch. The telephone is the second crutch. If you want to get something done, you've got to go out in person and grab it. Think of how much harder it is to say no to someone when he's staring you in the face. That's how you get your message across; that's how you create opportunity for yourself, whether it be getting a job, meeting someone new, or just building a foundation to create opportunity in the future.

Often I hear stories from people who are unhappy in the careers they've chosen and are longing to do something different, but they don't know where to start. I always tell them, "Look around, see what there is." By that I mean starting in your own workplace and looking around and seeing what other people are doing. If you see something you like, find out how you could do it, too. Maybe you're the mail clerk who sorts the letters as they come in from the post office. Maybe you'd like to be the guy who takes the letters from you and distributes them throughout the company. Making a change could be as simple as letting your supervisor know that if one of those positions opens up, you'd like a shot at it. Or even better yet, create a position where you could do a little of both and present it to your supervisor as a way to streamline the department.

Often a new opportunity is as close as that. It might not be the career switch you're looking for, but it could lead to other new opportunities as you get out in the company and see what those people are doing.

You don't have to stay pigeonholed in one place unless you really want to be there.

When I was about 10 I really wanted a new bike. But I didn't have enough money to buy a new bike, so I bought a used bike. And then I had transportation. I rode that bike over to Ft. Ord every day to shine shoes. And eventually, I had enough money to buy a new bike. I created the opportunity for myself.

And remember, just because a job isn't listed in the want ads doesn't mean that the job can't exist. Usually it means that nobody has thought of it yet. I always tell young people to diagram their dream job and then figure out a way to make it work in whatever arena they are trying to get into. Most often that means finding a way to convince a potential employer that you can save him money by hiring you. That's okay. In this economic climate, jobs anywhere are hard to get. I find that the most creative people are the ones who get hired. A secretary who also can help with the books because of his minor in accounting is a much better hire than someone who can just type. That person has created a position for himself—assistant to the president, instead of secretary to the president—and he created that opportunity by taking an extra few classes to make himself more marketable.

And know that there are always options to be negotiated. A friend of mine was offered a very good job that was going to require him to move 2000 miles. That wasn't attractive to him in the least, because his family didn't want to move, and he didn't want to be away from them. But he wanted the job. So he figured out a way that he could do the job without relocating by volunteering to take on extra responsibility on his side of the country, which would ultimately save the company money it normally would spend on travel. He made an extremely effective presentation to the company president, who wasted no time in saying he could stay where he was and still take the position.

Sometimes, however, creating your opportunity means simply taking a shot in the dark and hoping someone turns on the light. A high school student I know talked incessantly about wanting his own radio show when he finished college. He was smart and articulate, with a good radio-type voice and a drive to succeed that you don't often see in kids that age. I asked him one day, "Why wait until after college?"

"Nobody's going to hire a high school kid and give him a show," he answered.

"How do you know until you try?" I asked.

The kid thought about it and decided he had nothing to lose by approaching several of the stations in his city. He made a tape of interviews he had conducted for a class, wrote down a proposal of what the show would be and how it would be formatted, and knocked on doors, asking to meet with the program director. He was so convincing that it didn't take long before a tiny station that played country music decided to give him a shot at an early-morning slot it was trying to fill. It also helped that he was offering his services for free. But he didn't care that he wasn't getting paid. He had his own show, and he was just 17. He created an opportunity for himself when before there was none.

The postscript to this story is that his show was so successful—he worked long and hard to get some of the top athletes and sports personalities in the country to be his call-in guests—that within a year the show had advertising and he had a paycheck.

Just because you feel as if you are staring at a big wall doesn't mean there isn't a way around it or through it. Learn to think outside the norm, to see possibility when others see a dark hole. Figure out what it is you want and then find a way to achieve it by refusing to accept things just because they've always been a certain way.

Chad Pennington, our quarterback, wasn't highly recruited. The University of Tennessee said it would allow him to walk on, but that wasn't acceptable. Instead, he found a smaller school that wanted him badly, creating an opportunity for himself to play right away and succeed.

The same philosophy works in your personal life as well. If you want to meet someone special, it's important to create the opportunity to do so. If you don't, you might not ever meet the person you're hoping to meet. Join a running club or attend a photography seminar. Be assertive in introducing yourself to people and getting to know them and allowing them to get to know you. You may not find the person there, but at least you've created a productive space in which it could happen.

I find, too, that collecting the business cards and names and phone numbers of all kinds of people can greatly help you when you're trying to create something. A friend of mine wanted to start a charity that would raise money to fight skin cancer. She didn't know exactly where to start, but she remembered that she had met a man who worked for a cosmetic company a few years earlier and had kept his card. She phoned him, and within a few minutes, she had 1000 samples of sunblock to hand out as part of a campaign she began to urge young athletes to be careful of the dangers of the sun. Within a year, she had raised more than $100,000 through a charity fashion show sponsored by several major corporations that saw an opportunity to help someone make a difference in the lives of others.

Collecting cards also helps when you need someone else to create an opportunity for you. Coaches get fired all the time. It's one of the biggest hazards of the job because you're depending on wins to pay your rent. I find that the coaches who have lasted the longest are the ones who have not only collected the most business cards, but made the most phone calls and visits when they've needed a job. They were proactive in finding out who needed what assistant at what position, and then they went out and made a pitch to the head guy. It doesn't always work, but at least they were doing everything they could to create an environment in which they had a possibility.

Sitting home just wishing for something won't get it done.

Demand Discipline

When I took over the Jets, I told them first off that we were going to do things a certain way, and if we didn't do it that way, it meant we were not disciplined, and that was unacceptable to me. You have to have discipline—in every area of your life—if you are to achieve any kind of goals.

You have to exercise if you want to lose weight, you have to pay attention if you want to stay married (not that that's a discipline, but sometimes I can see how it might be one), and you have to keep making discipline a priority.

The Jets had been last in the league in turnovers the season before I got there. They weren't even close to the second-worst team. They were plus 18 and now we were plus 18, and that wasn't going to work for me.

I told them, "We are not going to beat ourselves. You start doing that, then I've got issues now. No, we are not turning this ball over, and we are not going to commit stupid penalties."

I am a detailed guy, and we were going to pay attention to details like that. I let them know that that was one of my top priorities, and I didn't care how long it took on a certain day to get that part of the game fixed. And that came down to discipline—making your hands wrap around that ball, making sure you tuck it in before you get hit, little things that require mindset and effort. That's what discipline is.

And you teach that by practicing like that each and every day. You make sure they pay attention to details. If you say, "Run from line to line," you make sure they touch that line or they do it over. There's no getting close to the line; there's no one inch from the line. If you're supposed to touch the line, you touch the line. If you only get close to the line, you only get close to the victories. If you say, "You will not cut corners running laps around the field," then you've got to make sure they don't cut the corners because cutting corners only gets you close.

If you say, "We will embrace diversity and each of you must come up with three candidates for our company who come from diverse backgrounds," then you make sure you check the list. Unless you demand that they do what you want them to do—even if it's little, or maybe because it's little—you will not change the environment in which they operate.

There is a reason why our military units operate as they do: It works. There is a reason why my father, no matter where we were, stopped the car and we saluted the flag on the base—even if we couldn't see it—when it was being raised or lowered or on any other occasion when we were to salute it. I remember clearly being in the middle of some street somewhere not even close to where the flag was and my father pulling over and beckoning me out of the car to salute. It was the discipline that was taught to him and handed down to me, and it's something I absolutely believe needs to exist wherever there is structure, and that's just about everywhere.

You can't go out wild and spend money if it's not in your budget. You can't go buy that coat or those shoes if you haven't set up the structure to allow that. Now, I'm the worst about budgets because I am lucky enough to have a job where I am making a good salary and a wife who knows about budgets and a son on a football scholarship. But I do know that your mind can always justify undoing the discipline. You give in; you buy a shirt that originally was $100 but now it's $50. But you weren't supposed to spend the $50. Your mind thinks you've done a good job because you've saved $50 when, in fact, you weren't supposed to spend the $50 in the first place.

Unless you have self-discipline, whether it's eating or exercising or spending money, you're in trouble. Because there's always something there to tempt you. There's a bag of chips or a donut or a sweater or a suit or a big piece of chocolate cake. Unless you have the inner strength to say, "No, I can't do that right now. That will take me off the road to achieving my goals," then you're never going to achieve them.

Sure you have to allow for setbacks. We're only human, and setbacks are part of life. Hopefully, though, we get back on track. Don't let setbacks derail you. If you eat that cake, get back on that treadmill as soon as you can. If you buy that sweater, take your lunch to work the next week until you get back into the discipline mode.

My best players are the ones who understand that they need to do certain things religiously, even in the off-season, if they are to come back into camp in the kind of shape we need them to be in. They're the ones who are running extra steps and sand dunes when nobody is asking them to, or lifting weights or working on speed training when nobody is watching. They're the ones who have the self-discipline to see what they need to do and then do it; believe it or not, there aren't that many who do that, despite the rewards if they do.

It's human nature to get lazy. I hear all the time about kids who take college classes that inspire them at first but then become too easy, and they lose interest. They aren't challenged, and they don't have the discipline to understand that they need to see the class through to get the grade, to get the credit they need to eventually graduate.

I also hear all the time about people who make excuses why they can't do something, or find reasons to justify why they do something else. "I'll do that report after I take a break," when, in fact, they've just come off a break. Or "I'll run twice as long tomorrow at the gym," when they know they're not in the kind of shape yet to run for that length of time. There's always "tomorrow." There's always "Monday." There are so many influences around that threaten to derail your goals. What you have to focus on is the discipline and convince yourself, because it's usually true, that the reward of being disciplined is so much greater.

Habits Form Who You Are, So Form Good Habits

First you form your habits, and then your habits form you. Whether you are becoming better or worse depends on what you do. Good habits and bad habits are the same. You've always got to check yourself on things, to say, "What did I do today, good and bad, that I did yesterday?" Sometimes you don't know. Sometimes things you repeat are bad. But you don't know it because you say, "It's just me." Sometimes I'll say something to somebody, and I'll say, "Why'd I say that? What was I thinking?" Then I do it two days in a row, and now I've got to fix it. I've got to apologize. It's easy to repeat things and before you know it they become who you are.

With the good things, that's a good thing. If you decide you want to run every day and it becomes a habit, then it's something that just gets done. It has to get done. You don't even think about it. It just gets done.

With the bad things, it's bad. Say you drink six beers and eat chips every night, and you do this again and again, and you start putting on weight, and you can't figure out why; well, look at the habit. Look at what you're doing.

You need to ask yourself, "What are you aspiring to become? What do you want?" Always look at yourself and say that the things you do in the dark will come to the light. If you've got to do them in the dark, what you're really saying is that you don't want them to come to the light. You should be able to do everything in the light. And if you want to change, you must deprogram yourself from the way you did things in the past and put yourself in a position to succeed.

My players fall into bad habits all the time. Maybe their footwork gets sloppy, or they start too low or too high. When I recognize it, we get them to practice the correction over and over and over until it's second nature. It's boring, but you need to get that habit corrected to the point where you don't think about it.

Second Quarter— Riding the Tide

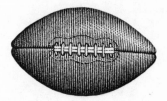

Character: the moral, ethical, and spiritual truth that reinforces your life and allows you to resist temptation and compromise.

–Unknown

In the second quarter of a football game, you're starting to get a feel for what's happening. Either it's good or it's bad. Sometimes you just have to ride it out until halftime, but take a good look at what's working and what's not. On your way to achieving your goals, there needs to be plenty of time for introspection, an evaluation of sorts of how things are going. We all need that in our personal lives as well, to make sure we're on the right path toward where we want to go.

Look Beyond the Mirror

A mirror reflects a man's face. But what he is really like is shown by the kind of friends he chooses. I challenge my players with this all the time by asking them to take a look at the guys they have around them. Are they guys who are looking for an easy ride? Or are they guys who are really looking out for you like a brother? When anyone finds some success, there are always people around who are looking to bring that person down—either intentionally or just by virtue of their character and motives.

A lot of top athletes have fallen because of the people they've chosen to be close with. Real friends are the people who don't have an agenda for being your friend. They care about your best interests as much as their own. They are the guys who take you home when you've been out too late, who come over and watch the game just to hang out.

They don't talk you into making the worst decision of your entire life.

The attraction of friendship can be alluring. Everyone wants to be accepted. But you have to stop and ask yourself why these people are suddenly in your life and what it is they're adding, or what it is they're trying to take away. Especially if you've made a name for yourself or made some money. Too many people want to latch onto that because they see easy street. A real friend never sees that street.

It's tough on a lot of the athletes who come from the inner city, where being part of a gang means staying alive. They leave to go on to the NBA or the NFL, and their guys back home expect to either come with them or, at least, share in the wealth. Guys tell me all the time how they sometimes feel obligated to maintain friendships with the guys back home, to give them money and respect; otherwise, they get their "ghetto pass revoked." It's a tough line to walk. Do you turn your back on those guys and risk alienating your old neighborhood forever, or do you maintain the relationship and risk your career and, possibly, your life?

I heard about a speech by a young man who said he had once been a gangbanger. His friends lured him into the life even though he knew it was wrong. He ended up deciding to go with them one night even though his mother and another friend, who had gotten wind of his decision, tried to talk him down. He insisted that he had no choice, that these guys were his friends and they wouldn't let anything bad happen to him. He found his buddies, got into the car, and crossed that imaginary line into enemy gang territory. Within minutes gunshots rang out; they sped away, but not before the young man's best friend was killed. He died in his arms. Eight years and a prison sentence later, the young man was speaking to a group of kids at a youth center. He told them he had been a gangbanger—a gangbanger for five minutes.

"Some of my friends tried to talk me out of it, but my other friends were talking me into it. I wanted to be cool. I wanted them to like me. Five minutes into it, my best friend got shot, and he died. Five minutes. He was the friend who had asked me whether I was a baby or a man. A real man would have said no and walked away, and a real friend wouldn't have asked."

If your friends are dragging you into trouble, then they are not your friends. Be careful whom you trust. The spotlight attracts all kinds of insects and vermin. Make sure the people you are around have as much to lose as you do if trouble erupts. Find people who share your interests, your passions, your way of living. That doesn't mean they all need to be your clones. In fact, diversity in thinking can be a valuable learning tool.

My best friends, besides my wife, are the men who mentored me and the men I mentor. John Lynch remains the best athlete I've ever coached and one of the best men I've ever met. John's the godfather of our son, Marcus. That's how much Lia and I think of him. The way he approaches life is similar to the way I approach it. We know we're far from perfect, but we also try to minimize our mistakes by reading the Bible and walking the walk together.

I can look at a player, and if he is surrounded by people who make him uneasy in the company of either my staff or myself, then I know that young man could be headed for trouble. I tell them that you can learn from history or you can be part of it. The people you want to be around are those who share your goals for happiness and success.

Don't Point Fingers

When you point a finger at someone, three fingers always point back at you. Blaming someone else for something is the easiest thing in the world to do and is usually wrong. When you're involved in something that fails or in something in which a mistake is made, more often than not, you're to blame, too. It's just easier to blame the other guy, and this is a device that most people can see right through.

Often in football, and in other sports, too, the outcome of a game comes down to a final play. Somebody makes a field goal or a penalty kick or a last-second three-pointer, or somebody hits a grand slam with two out in the bottom of the ninth. It happens, and somebody wins and somebody loses because of somebody's action or inaction. But you can't think of it like that. The outcome wasn't really decided by one final play. It was simply a culmination of everything that had happened in the game before that final moment. Sure, everyone loves the drama of a last-second victory, and everyone dreads the drama of a last-second defeat—and it's all you'll read about in the newspapers or see on TV the next day. But it's really what led to that final play's being the deciding factor that caused the outcome of the game: The offense turned the ball over too many times, the players fouled in the box, the batters weren't patient. A team never lets a play come down to a last-second situation, in which one person decides it all. Even if he made the shot, I say he didn't win the game—the team put him in a position to hit a shot that won the game. He surely didn't win it on his own. And if he misses the shot, he didn't lose the game for the team, because the team shouldn't have had to rely on that shot to win. That's why you can't blame him; you can't point fingers.

You shouldn't point fingers at anyone. Say you've worked really hard on a project with a couple of people in the office. It's supposed to be a joint effort, the results reflective of the coming together of some good minds. Except the project fails. It's a dud, and you're really worried about how that will reflect on you. So you defend yourself by saying, "Well, he didn't do this and she didn't do that," failing to take the responsibility as a group for the things that went wrong. The real failure is that your group didn't act as a team to make sure that what needed to get done got done. Usually it's not just one person's fault, even if that person completely dropped the ball and flaked out. It was the responsibility of the group to know that that person was flaking out and take action, either kicking him out of the group or making him aware that he needed to do his part or figuring some other way out. Nobody in a supervisory position wants to hear why something didn't get done, or why something didn't work; they want results. Period. They say, "Don't tell me what the problem is. Find me a solution."

I've seen players on teams blame one another for missed assignments, for getting burned by an opponent, even for losses. This disharmony usually comes when a team is losing, but I've also seen it when a player has an agenda—perhaps an incentive for making a certain amount of interceptions or tackles. If something doesn't go his way, his first reaction, because he's self-absorbed to begin with, is to blame someone else for blocking the path, when, in fact, it was his own inability to get the job done.

Even when someone else is truly at fault, pointing it out to her rarely gets the productive results you ultimately want. Sometimes that person does need to be called out, but it is the way in which you do it that determines whether you'll only anger her or whether you'll fix the problem and move on.

Say two of the people in your group are responsible for monitoring a certain web site and are to let you know when relevant new documents are filed. You work through a day, and the next morning you are stunned to find out that they didn't read through one of the new documents in its entirety and thus failed to bring it to your attention because they had dismissed it as something unimportant. You find out the next day that the relevant material was toward the end of the document, and you're enraged. How could they be so irresponsible as not to read the entire document? Before you launch into a tirade about their incompetence, stop and ask yourself what you want to accomplish. Do you want to create a scene and point fingers, or do you want to fix the problem and move on? You also have to ask yourself what you could have done to avoid the problem.

The people in your group are responsible for monitoring the web site, but you, as the group's leader, are responsible as well for reading all the documents posted there. The fact that they didn't call the relevant matter to your attention is their fault, yes, but your fault, as a supervisor, was not seeing that they did things correctly. You need to trust the people with whom you work, but you also have to realize that you are as responsible as they are when things go wrong. The effective way to fix the problem and move on is to frame your conversation with the group so as to accept some of the blame yourself, and then make your point. "I was wrong not to read that entire document myself," you say, for example, followed by, "Next time, can you guys make sure you read through it all the way and make sure I do, too?" That is so much more effective than saying,

"You guys blew it." All that creates is bad feelings. Assigning yourself some of the blame allows them to realize they made a mistake, correct it, and move on.

Pointing fingers in a relationship never works, either. Not if you want it to last. Even if you believe the other person is wrong, as in the business examples just given, there is a way to go about fixing the problem without assigning blame. The wash didn't get done, the mail wasn't put in the right place, the dry cleaning didn't get picked up. Blaming your spouse isn't going to solve the problem, even if it was his responsibility to do those things. Blame him and the fingers point back at you. Maybe you should have offered to take some of the load off. What could you have done differently to see that those things got done? Maybe it's something as simple as making an extra stop on the way home from work.

Before assigning blame, it is always best to ask yourself what you could have done differently yourself that might have avoided the error or mistake in the first place.

Not All Money Is Good Money

When someone's offering you money for something, you need to find out whom you are accepting it from and why he wants to give it to you. I've had opportunities throughout my career to make more money as a coach. The head guy has come after me, offering me a raise and a promotion to coordinator to come join his team, but I've turned him down because it wasn't worth it to me. I wasn't going to sell my soul by giving in to someone else's philosophy or beliefs that I didn't agree with. The money might have been a little better. The title might have been a little better. But for me, that wasn't my goal.

My goal, all along, has been to be a head coach, and unless I saw taking the coordinator spot as being a workable situation that would help me get to the next level, I didn't think it was something I could do, especially if the head guy and I didn't agree on some very key philosophies.

When I was in Tampa, life was very good. For me to leave there for anything other than a head-coaching job, it would have to have been an unbelievable opportunity. I enjoyed the environment there, I agreed with how Tony Dungy approached things, and I knew I was learning a lot about becoming a head coach just by watching him. Our son, Marcus, was nearby, playing high school football and the time we were able to spend together really meant a lot to Lia and me.

Money doesn't motivate me. It never has. Even now, I don't have a checkbook. Lia takes care of all that stuff. Most days I've got about seven dollars in my pocket. I don't dream of obtaining material wealth. Big houses and cars and boats and diamonds and furs have never been something I wanted.

If money is the goal, then however much you acquire, it can never be enough. And once people find out you're doing something for the money only, they know they can buy you. And then you stand for nothing. Everybody needs money; I understand that. But how that money is acquired is what's important.

Drug money is bad. Prostitution money is bad. Money made on false pretenses is bad. Look at how many people are in jail now because they let money guide their ambition. Executives, CEOs, presidents of top companies—people who appeared to have everything they would ever need in their lives are now spending time as common criminals. The more wealth they acquired, the more they needed. You can't take money that gets you in more trouble than not having any money at all. Feeding my family is the most important thing in my life, but taking illegal money to do it isn't an option. You get caught and sent to jail, and then what does your family do?

People who spend time obsessing over what they don't have don't see what they do have. If you're spending all your time at the office so that you can make that overtime check to buy your son some fancy gadget he wants, then you're cheating your son of what's really important: time with his dad. And you're cheating yourself out of time spent with your son. I heard someone say that no one has ever heard a guy on his deathbed say he wished he had spent more time at the office.

We all want a bigger paycheck; that's a fact. Because most of us equate that paycheck with our worth. We want to feel that our work is valuable and important. But equating that paycheck with our worth isn't always right. Look at the paychecks of some of the people who matter most in our lives. Firemen, policemen, nurses, teachers, paramedics—they are perhaps the lowest-paid members of our society. And yet, we couldn't survive without them. How is it that the guy who saves your home from a fire, or keeps you from being robbed, or drives you to the emergency room makes so much less than the head of some company who will probably never touch your life? The Fortune 500? Most of us have never even heard of these guys and probably will never need to know them. That doesn't mean that what they do isn't worthy or isn't important, but for most of us, their jobs have no direct impact on our lives. Money does not equal worth. Worth is what you feel inside from the effort you give to do your best in your job and in your life.

Never Look Down on Anybody Unless You're Helping Him Up

My dad used to say this all the time, but it was Tony Dungy who showed me firsthand the importance of people helping one another along the way to achieving their own success. It's not so much giving back (although that's important, too) as giving someone a leg up. Success is so much more meaningful when you realize you've used it to help someone else achieve success, too.

Tony and I met when we were both playing college all-star games back in 1976. Back then, you'd play in the Hula Bowl, and then the same teams would go to the Japan Bowl. We all traveled together for two weeks, and for some reason, Tony and I just hit it off. We weren't big going-out guys, so we hung out a lot together and started talking. Tony was intriguing to me because he was a quarterback, a black quarterback, and there weren't many back then. We talked a lot about race and sports, but mainly we talked about our desires and dreams to make a life in professional football.

It's a good thing we hit it off, because I unwittingly ruined his chances to be the hero of the Japan Bowl. We played on opposite teams, and Tony was leading his team down the field in the final minutes and would have won the game, except he threw a pass at our 15-yard line that got tipped, and I ended up intercepting it, and we won. He told me afterward, "I could have been MVP and you, my new friend, go out and intercept that pass." He jokes that he's been mad at me ever since.

We both ended up undrafted rookie defensive backs (he knew he'd have to move positions to play at the next level), and we stayed in touch. After we finished playing, we ended up on the same staff in Kansas City. I had gotten an internship with the Chiefs in 1989 while I was coaching defensive backs at San Jose State. The internship was part of the NFL's minority intern program, and it helped create a lot of jobs for young minority coaches. I thought it was a great opportunity, so I joined the Chiefs' staff, where Tony was coaching the defensive backs. When he left in 1992 to be Dennis Green's defensive coordinator with the Vikings, I got his job with the Chiefs. And when Tony got the Tampa Bay job, I found my phone ringing and his voice on the other end of the line saying, "Herm, I don't want to put any pressure on you, but I really need you."

That's all I needed to hear. I knew Tony would teach me the things I needed to know to become a head coach myself; I just didn't know how much he would teach me and how much he would help me.

One of the first things he put me in charge of was the discipline. When a guy got into trouble, I was the guy who laid down the law about how guys were to conduct themselves. Tony knew it was the hardest thing to learn on your way to becoming a head coach and something I needed do firsthand. He said one of the reasons he did that for me was that Dennis Green had done it for him. Denny spent extra time with Tony just about every day helping him get ready. Tony said he wanted to pass it on to me, and there was nobody happier than Tony when I finally got my shot with the Jets.

It's something I am passing on, too, to my assistants who have head-coaching aspirations. Giving somebody a leg up isn't climbing the ladder for them. It's passing knowledge to them that they can use to get to where you are and beyond. It's seeing someone walk in the door who reminds you of you when you were just starting out.

I have a friend who is a reporter who makes a point of visiting the school newspaper at every college campus she goes to. She takes time to get to know some of the staff members and often maintains the relationship. She told me she does it because she remembers how much it meant to her when someone else did that back when she was starting out.

"I see myself in those kids' eyes," she told me. "They have that same eagerness, that same wide-eyed expression, and the hunger to learn everything they can about what it is I do and how I got there."

She gives them her contact numbers and tries to guide them in the right direction. "So many of them tell me I'm much more down-to-earth than they thought I'd be," she said. "It's because I treat them as equals in the profession, even though they've barely begun. I don't look down on them or tower above. I just figure out how I can help them accomplish their goals."

Not everyone is like that. Jobs are hard to find these days. A lot of people would be threatened by the eagerness of some college kid who would give his left arm to get your job. Jealousy is rampant in any workforce. It turns rational, caring people into caricatures. They become what they never think is possible, spending their time trying to bring someone else down in the eyes of others and becoming blinded to what they, themselves, have achieved.

In 2002 Tony and I made history as the first black head coaches to face each other in the NFL playoffs. We both had believed that if we worked hard and did the right things, someone would give us the opportunity. I knew Tony was thankful for his opportunity, and I was thankful for mine. It was a step in the right direction toward what the National

Football League is trying to adopt. Tony never saw helping me as a threat to the success he had found. Or, if he did, he never told me that or acted that way. And there was no reason for him to be threatened or jealous—he was already so accomplished and secure in his own abilities. Even when Tampa Bay fired him, he was confident that something else would come along. And, thankfully, it did quickly.

Before the Colts scooped him up, though, I found myself with Tony and Dennis Green, who had just left the Vikings, at a housing project in Washington, D.C., to help celebrate Martin Luther King Day. It dawned on me that I was the only one of the three of us who had a job, which made me the only black coach in the NFL at the time. It felt strange standing next to the two men who were most responsible for helping me get ready for the Jets job. It wasn't long after, though, that Indianapolis hired Tony and Denny became the head coach of the Arizona Cardinals. Good things come around to people who help one another.

I have another friend who related to me a story with a similar message. It seems that some time ago, she showed great kindness to a man who was working on a project on which she had done extensive research. She had never met the man, but when he called, she opened up her files to him and brainstormed with him for weeks about how he could go about developing his project. She didn't hear from him again for 10 years, and when she saw him, she couldn't quite place him.

"He looked familiar, but I didn't remember how I knew him," she said.

But he did. And he then introduced himself as her new boss and gave her an immediate promotion.

What You Do in the Dark Will Come to the Light

This is a phrase from the New Testament and, to me, it applies to many different things. One afternoon I walked into our meeting room at Jets camp and told it to my guys. "What you do in the dark will come to the light, boys. You gotta remember that." Well, that sent them reeling. They all went, "Oh, man . . ." Every single guy was saying to himself, "What did I do last night?" You could see their brains at work, thinking, "What did I do in the dark? What does he know about what I did in the dark? What is he talking about? Is he talking about me?" I guarantee it made them think.

What it means is that what you do when nobody is watching will surface at some point when someone is watching. And that means both the good things and the bad. If you're working out and eating right when nobody is watching, eventually someone's going to notice you've lost weight or become more fit. If you're always drinking and staying out late away from the job, eventually the job will notice that you're tired, run down, and ineffective.

When I had issues growing up, I wasn't very effective in practice or in class. If I was dealing with problems with girls or friends or the trouble they were trying to pull me into and I was trying to listen in the classroom and then listen to the coach, it just didn't work. I couldn't deal with problems outside the classroom and off the field and be effective in the classroom and on the field. Fortunately, I figured out early in my life what it was I wanted to do, and I found a way to rid myself of the problems that were threatening my progress. I also found a way to say no to the temptations that lure a young man to the wrong side of the street.

Once I knew that going that way wasn't preparing me the right way to accomplish my goals, then it was clear what I should and should not do.

Now, that's not to say I wasn't on the edge at times. What I learned, though, was as soon as my friends led me to that edge, to turn and go in the other direction. I knew if they were going to Fifth Street, I had to check out by Fourth Street. Becoming a professional football player wasn't just a goal for me, it was a passion, and I wasn't about to let vice and foolishness deter me in my quest. Once I got my issues cleaned up, I was able to focus on the right things I needed to do, and I got things done.

What I tell my players is what I learned way back then: that until you get your outside problems cleaned up, you'll never accomplish what you want to accomplish. Your problems might be partying a little too much or way too much, or even staying up too late watching TV at night and not getting enough sleep. I think all players understand that issues will show up at some point. They all think they're fooling everybody until one day their issues show up on the field. They're a step slow, or they're winded early, or their reactions are delayed. And once their issues show up on the field, then their issues become my issues.

"Because," I tell them, "I just let my team down because I trusted you to go out there and play, and you didn't come through because you didn't clean up your issues away from the game. So now I don't trust you, and if I don't trust you, you can't play."

My players expect me to put the best players on the field. And those are the players who have prepared themselves mentally and physically in the dark and in the light. I am accountable to the team for making the right decisions. And if what some guy is doing behind the scenes isn't conducive to his being prepared, then we'll all find out soon enough.

This is all about making sure your life is in order to do what it is that you want to do—doing whatever it takes to get yourself ready for the task at hand.

During my first day of class at Berkeley, one of the professors told us, "Here are the books you should read. I don't take roll. I don't care if you come to class. All you are required to do is take the midterm and the final. That's all you've got to do." At first I was thinking, "Wow, this is great! I don't even have to go to class." But I soon realized that if I didn't go to class and I didn't do the reading, then I wasn't going to pass the midterm or the final. If I wasn't prepared, it would come to light on that report card.

I've had players show up for training camp who tried hard to convince me that they had worked hard during the off-season and were ready for camp. "Oh, yeah, coach. I ran sand hills. I was in the weight room. I was a workout freak. I'm ready to go." Halfway through the first day, they're gassed. That's the easiest example of showing how what you do—or don't do—in the dark will come to the light. There is just no way to fake being in shape. Mia Hamm, the great soccer player on the U.S. Women's World Cup team, said, "Great soccer players are made when nobody is watching." She was referring to her relentless workouts during the off-season, and it applies to everything else, too.

Say you're trying to lose weight and you're on a program that is bound to help you lose that weight, which most likely involves eating less of the bad foods and exercising more. So you're walking or running, you're getting some weight work in and eating healthy food, and pretty soon you start seeing results. So you're happy about that and proud of yourself and thrilled with what's going on, and that's a good thing. But maybe one night you decide, well, maybe just this once, I'm going to skip that workout or eat those brownies over there because they sure look good and nobody's around, so why not? And then the next night it's something else. But nobody's watching, right? And you're still down a few pounds, and you're feeling good, so why not? But then gradually it becomes a habit, and you keep making excuses. Pretty soon all that weight has come back on, and you don't know why, and none of your friends know why because all they've seen is you trying hard, working out, and ordering the right stuff when you go to lunch. But you know why, really. You know it's what you were doing when they weren't around that has sabotaged your efforts.

The best thing I can do as a coach is prepare my team to come out on Sunday, where they will be judged. What we do in the dark comes to the light every Sunday.

The best thing I can do as a man is make sure that what I do in the dark is something I am not afraid to do in the light.

Make Everybody Accountable

My players are professional football players. To me, that carries deep responsibility. There is a standard they need to live by and live up to. I tell them all the time that if they don't live up to that standard, there will be times when I'm going to need to issue more than a verbal correction. I let them know early on that there may be times when we have to withhold privileges or establish penalties to hold immature people accountable. You can talk all you want and say you're going to punish someone for wrong actions, but talk is cheap; real consequences lend force to words.

I don't believe in a lot of rules. I believe in setting high expectations and making sure each individual is aware of what is expected of him. I expect him to handle himself professionally at all times, and if he doesn't, then we're going to have issues. I don't care who he is.

John Abraham is one of our best players. During the 2003 season, he made a serious mistake in judgment by driving after he had been out drinking. He was arrested for driving under the influence, and he had to spend the night in jail and miss practice. We were 0–4 at the time, and we needed him badly, but I knew, and everyone else knew, too, what I was going to do. One of our rules is, don't miss practice. Don't be late and don't miss practice. If you do, there will be consequences.

We all make mistakes, but that could have been a critical mistake for him, for his career, for the people involved. You can't take that lightly, and you can't forgive the fact that it affected his ability to come to work that day. Nobody on my team gets a hall pass. The rules and standards were already set. I told my players, "This is the way it goes. You make decisions every day whether to go down road A or road B. With every decision, there's consequences. Some are good. Some are bad. You get to make the choice."

The way I saw it, John had put himself before the football team. And once someone does that, then I've got serious problems. Guys kept saying to me, "The league hasn't done anything, so maybe you shouldn't either." That didn't matter to me. The league doesn't run this football team. I do, and I set the policy.

Now, that doesn't mean I don't have compassion. I knew the first thing I had to do was help the player and make sure he was okay, and then I had to help the football team. I knew what I was going to do, but I waited to do it. John came up into my office, and I said, "You know what I have to do, right?" He knew. I didn't fine him; I wasn't going to take his money. Why would I do that? The league will do that. What I did was deactivate him. The team rule was, you have to be here for practice. So he wasn't going to play. Simple as that. He missed practice because he chose to do something; he chose road B when he should have chosen road A, and it landed him in jail and on the deactive list.

Nobody thought I would do it. Everyone was saying that I wouldn't bench my best player. Not when we were 0–4. Heck, I told them, we were 0-and-4 with John Abraham; we can certainly lose a fifth with or without him. I said, "We don't need this guy. We're going to play together as a team with players who choose the right road." John understood. He knew he had made a mistake and now had consequences to pay. It sent a big message to the rest of the team, too. If I'm holding John accountable, make no mistake, I'm going to hold all of them accountable.

Often the person who has to dole out punishment or consequences feels bad about doing it. I felt bad that John had made a mistake, but I didn't feel bad about deactivating him because he knew the rules. Sometimes it's not so clear-cut, though.

Say you check your bank account one day, and you find that your housekeeper has taken one of your checks and has illegally written it to herself and has cashed it. The amount was only $30, as she tearfully tells you after you find out, and she used it to pay the rest of her rent, which was way over-due. You feel bad, she feels bad, and maybe you let it go, and then where are you? Always looking over your shoulder, always wondering what is going to happen next. No, you can't let it go. She made a decision, and what she did was wrong, and there have to be consequences because that's the way society works. The real problem, you tell her, is that she never told you about the check; she never left a note or a voice message, and she didn't get it repaid before you found out, as she said she had been planning to.

It hurts you to fire her, but she must be held accountable for her action. What does it say to your daughter if you just let it go? What does it say to everyone around you? Every decision a person makes has ramifications. You had to fire her because otherwise you are telling her she is above the rules. You are showing your kids that there are exceptions, that not everyone has to pay the price for doing something wrong. You are telling yourself that the rules don't matter. Society doesn't work that way.

I had to deactivate my best player. Maybe you have to demote your best assistant, or ground your kid for lying. You do it not because you enjoy it, but because it's the right thing to do. In the end, you hope the person learns from his mistake and can move on to a better place. That's what you hope for. If you don't do anything, then you just might be keeping that person back.

Don't Waste Energy on the Unknowns

Going into something new, whether it is football or anything else in life, too many people waste a lot of energy on the unknowns. They spend all their time trying to figure things out, such as, "What is he going to say?" or "What does he want to do?" People get far too wrapped up in anticipation:

"What if this happens?" and "What am I supposed to do if this happens?" That's a lot of wasted energy. People think I have a lot of energy, but I don't. I don't have a lot to waste. Concentrate on what you know and what you do really well, and don't worry about the rest.

Halftime—Making Adjustments

When a man is able to take abuse with a smile, he is worthy to become a leader.

—Nachman of Bratslav

You go into that locker room at halftime, and either you're happy with what has happened or you're not. If you're not, you'd better find out quick what went wrong in the first half and correct it. If you're trying to achieve something and something has gone wrong, you've got to fix that, too. Life is all about making adjustments, solving problems, navigating your way through issues and circumstances that sometimes are out of your control. Often it's how you look at something that shapes it in your mind. We all have troubled times; it's how you react to them that counts. Becoming an effective leader sometimes means making adjustments to the message when the message isn't working.

Hit It and Deal with It

Life is filled with speed bumps. You're cruising right along, and then you hit one. Some are bigger than others; that's a fact. What's important is not that you hit the speed bump; it's how you navigate it. So you hit one—then what do you do? Do you wallow in self-pity, or do you deal with it?

Top athletes have to learn to live with mini-speed bumps every day. Baseball players, on the average, fail four times for every time they get a hit. Runners rarely post personal-best times; more often than not, their times are below their best. Those athletes have learned that it's how they react to those failures or mistakes that's important. A soccer player might get stripped of the ball, but if he chases the guy back down the field and alters his pass, then he's made something good out of something bad.

Facing and dealing with speed bumps and working through them, no matter how large or small they are, will give you the inner strength to keep going. Every case is different. But in the end, every result is the same. Deal with obstacles, learn from them, and refuse to give in.

Say your son gets hurt playing sports. He's a top high school athlete who is being recruited by a bunch of colleges and it's his senior year, and just before it begins, he tears his ACL, and there goes the season. He's going to need surgery and rehab, and he's now going to miss out on so much. He's devastated; you're devastated. But what do you do? Do you sit there and cry and mourn what was lost? You can't. How does that help him to get where he wants to go, which is to college to play football?

I always say that when something bad happens, you can feel bad; it's natural to feel bad, but feel bad for about five minutes. Then let it go because feeling bad doesn't bring anything to the table other than feeling bad. You've got to leave it behind and focus on the future. Okay, your son is hurt. He's going to need surgery, and things are going to be pretty rough for him for a while. Instead of feeling bad, ask yourself, "What can I do to help him get back on track? How can I help him?" You can help him by making a plan and showing him how you're going to tackle this problem, and you can reassure him that everything is going to be fine. Not only will this help him get through a tough time, but you've just now given him a valuable lesson that will guide him through life. Problems creep up all the time. Sometimes they smack you straight in the face. And it's tough. Sometimes it's really tough.

We lost our quarterback to injury the third preseason game of the 2003 season. Chad Pennington had put on a show in 2002, and expectations were high. But he dislocated his thumb, and the diagnosis was he'd be out for 12 weeks. Sure I felt bad. He felt bad. We all felt bad. But I knew feeling bad wasn't going to win us any games. What we needed was to deal with that speed bump. I gathered my guys together and said not to worry. "We've got a quarterback. We've got a good quarterback. Vinny Testaverde has won a bunch of games for us, and he's going to step in and do it again."

We felt bad for Chad, but by shifting the focus from feeling bad for him to feeling good about Vinny, we accomplished a lot of things. Chad was able to stop feeling he had let the team down, which is as destructive an emotion as there is, and start thinking about doing everything he could to heal because he knew that we believed we'd be okay without him. And the team stopped thinking they were doomed because Chad was out and started thinking about how they could help Vinny.

On a much more personal note, my wife, Lia, was diagnosed with diabetes a few years ago. We were stunned. Lia is probably the healthiest person I know. She eats right; she works out all the time. But here's the doctor telling us she's got diabetes and is going to have to monitor her blood sugar and come in for tests and keep a very close watch on her health. It was frightening to both of us—especially to Lia. At first she didn't really understand the disease, nor did I. Lia thought she might die, or at least lose years off her life. But once we got educated on how controllable diabetes is by the use of an insulin pump and other wonders of modern science, it was much easier to feel okay about things.

Still, she was terrified of having to test her blood sugar every day, and I knew I wouldn't be around all the time to do it for her. So I pulled myself together, grabbed one of those needles, and pricked my own finger to show her it was no big deal. It made her laugh, and it wasn't long before this speed bump was way in the rearview mirror.

The hardest thing I ever had to go through, the biggest speed bump in my life, was when my dad passed away. I was only 23, and I had just finished my rookie year with the Eagles. My dad wasn't sick; he wasn't in bad health or anything. One day he went out to run an errand, and within 20 minutes after he left the house, the hospital was calling to say he'd been in a car accident after passing out while driving. I rushed to the hospital to find out what had happened, but the doctors didn't really know. He seemed so tired to me. All he kept saying was that everything was going to be fine, and I really did think everything was going to be fine. But it wasn't. He died that day.

The last thing my father told me was that I had to be strong. "Make sure your mother and your sister are okay," he said. And then he was gone. It was devastating to all of us. And confusing. He was gone, and I was sitting there saying, "What am I supposed to do?"

I had achieved my goal of playing professional football, but now I was responsible for my mother and my sister, and I wondered what that meant, how it would all fit. My dad had seen me play against the Los Angeles Rams; in fact, he saw my first interception—picking off Joe Willie Namath— and I saw after the game how proud he was of me. I thought about things for a long time, and I came to the conclusion that I could do both—take care of my family and continue playing football. I felt that that was what my dad would want me to do: to make sure my sister and my mother were taken care of and then move on with my career.

I did everything I could think of around the house to make sure it would be easy for them to live there without my dad. I even pulled up the lawn and put down rock so they wouldn't have to deal with the front lawn. I took care of how the bills were going to be paid and the car maintained—all the things that my dad did, I figured out a way to get them done, or at least make them as easy as possible for my mom to deal with. And once I knew my mother and my sister were okay, I went back to work. My heart was heavy, but I knew it was what my dad would have wanted me to do.

When Green Bay Packers quarterback Brett Favre lost his father during the 2003 season, it reminded me so much of what I had gone through 25 years earlier. It brought back some of the pain, but it also reminded me that what I had done way back then was the right thing to do. I was hoping Brett would find that answer, too, and he did—he turned in one of his best performances ever in a Monday night game a day after burying his dad. Later I read that he had said he felt his father was with him that night. I know mine is with me now, too.

The heat of hard times is designed to improve us. How we react to heartache and obstacles and problems and tough situations defines us as sons, daughters, mothers, or fathers, and as individuals. It gives each of us a chance to challenge ourselves and pass lessons on to others. It gives us an opportunity to do something right. It allows us to turn something devastating into something wonderful.

I believe God never tries to trip us up, but he does allow tough circumstances to surface to build our character and maturity. Two of the most beautiful metals in this world are silver and gold. I learned that they are refined by intense heat, which forces the impurities to float to the top. The impurities are then skimmed off to improve the quality of the metal. In the same way, suffering through problems and situations allows the moral impurities in our characters to surface. Then we are able to see them and skim them off, too.

I know that before anyone can really enjoy success, he must deal with speed bumps. They mean nothing as long as something is gained by how he reacts to them and how he solves the problems they create.

Simplify the Message

I have come to realize that anybody who is listening to somebody else really hears only 10 percent of what the other person is saying. The other 90 percent vanishes into thin air. So you've got to get your message out there as quickly as you can and in such a way that people understand what it is you're saying and then remember it. Find a phrase or a statement that emphasizes your point so that when they walk away, they'll say, "Oh, I can remember that."

That's what this book is filled with—simple phrases that I hope will trigger the message behind them. I think that if you break the message down into the simplest terms, anyone can understand it. If it's too complicated, it's no good. Simplify and let the meaning surface.

Throughout my playing career, I found myself in meeting room after meeting room where a coach would talk on and on and on. He never realized that half the guys in the room were asleep or thinking about something else. He must have liked the sound of his voice and the idea that he was in front of the group and had a platform. Or so he thought.

A lot of managers believe that the more they talk, the more they get across. I believe it's just the opposite. When I became a position coach in Kansas City, I never kept my players in a meeting room for more than 20 minutes without a break. It used to drive Marty Schottenheimer nuts. Every 15 or 20 minutes I'd say, "Take a break, men." Marty came to me one day and said, "Why are you always giving these guys breaks?"

I said, "Coach, are you kidding? You want me to keep the defensive backs in this room for an hour and a half? These guys? These guys are hyper-mental. You can't keep these guys sitting in a room that long."

I was a player. I know how players think. Most of them, especially defensive backs, are on a sugar high their whole lives. Now, if you go out on the field with them, that's different. I'm throwing them the ball, we're running routes, and I'm showing them the same thing I was talking about in the classroom. Suddenly they're saying, "Oh, I see what you mean, coach."

But keep them in the classroom for an hour and a half and they won't learn a thing.

It's something I've carried over to the Jets, too. I won't let my assistants keep their guys in a meeting for more than 20 minutes. More often than not, they're out in 10. If you keep them too long, you lose them. Their minds start wandering. They start thinking about everything but whatever it is you're trying to get them to think about. If you spend too much time talking about whatever scheme they're going to face or employ, I guarantee that guys will start thinking about what they're going to have for dinner, whom they're going to see after practice, or what's going on with their kids. And once you've lost them, it's nearly impossible to get them back.

I find that if you keep your message focused, keep it concise, and keep it brief, then you have a much better chance of making it stick.

Your wife can give you 20 minutes on why she wants you to pick up the dry cleaning, and even though I believe in explaining the why to people, it's not something most husbands need to know in regard to actually picking up the dry cleaning. Usually, a quick, "Please pick up the dry cleaning," is enough. "Please pick up the dry cleaning and I will make you a wonderful dinner" probably is even more effective.

Some of the best public service ads I've seen are the ones involving teenagers and drug use. A simple, "Talk to your kids about drugs" has been a very successful campaign aimed at parents, who need to understand that the communication lines between them and their children need to be open. It's a phrase anybody can remember, and it's something that surfaces easily as your teenager is headed out the door to a party. Another one I remember is the picture of an egg. "This is your brain," the voice says. The shot cuts to an egg frying in a pan: "This is your brain on drugs." You get the idea right smack in the face. It's something I think kids can easily relate to because it's short and it involves a pretty powerful visual. When I really want my players to get something, I flash it on the overhead screen. The power of hearing a short message and seeing it at the same time makes this a valuable tool.

I understand that some people can't operate like that. They don't feel that they're making their point or delivering their message unless they expound on every single little detail that leads them to what it is. They spend too much time explaining things that aren't relevant and, more often than not, go in the other person's one ear and out the other.

A coworker is trying to tell you that she needs an extra day to finish her report. But instead of saying, "I need an extra day to finish my report," she launches into her troubles with her kids, her dog, her car, and the people who were supposed to deliver the supplies, and how she couldn't find the phone number of the research assistant who was supposed to phone her, and you're running for the door to get away before she is able to tell you what it is she needs. Sometimes you need an explanation, but I've found that explanations get lost amid all the words that go into them. Simple is much easier and far more effective.

I once heard about a guy who worked as a consultant. I was told that his theories and ideas were good, but his presentations were so long and laborious that people couldn't stand the man by the second day. They started at 8 a.m., and they got a few 10-minute breaks throughout the day and a half-hour for lunch—which was brought into the room where the seminar was being held. The guy kept saying he had so much material to cover and not enough time, so he felt he had to utilize every minute he had with the group. As a result, his teachings were largely wasted.

You can't tell me that a consultant who keeps people in a room for eight hours without major breaks because he doesn't want to waste time is getting his message across effectively. In fact, he's doing just the opposite: He's alienating the group he's been hired to reach. These were young, aggressive professionals who were ready to listen to what he said, but they couldn't get through the first day without tuning him out at various points. An effective communicator knows his audience; he also knows a way to communicate so that his audience comes away with some sort of understanding of what he is delivering.

I try to boil down everything I say so that a five-year-old can understand it. That's the surest way I know to get your message to stick.

Pare Down the Goal

Sometimes the big picture is so overwhelming that you can hardly see your hands in front of you. When that's the case, you need to step back, take a deep breath, and break down what is overwhelming you into workable parts to make it more manageable.

When I first got into the coaching business, I would look at what the head coach had to do, and I couldn't imagine having to deal with all the things he had to deal with. And yet, when the opportunity came for me to become the head coach of the Jets, I jumped in with both feet.

I came in knowing that it was a great honor, that I had achieved something I had set out to do a long time ago. Looking back now, I remember getting a lot of pats on the back and a lot of handshakes, but feeling the loneliest I've ever felt once I walked into my office that first day and closed the door behind me. All of a sudden I realized, "Hey, I'm the head coach. Now what do I do?" Everyone around me had walked away and I was by myself, and all the plans and ideas that had been rushing through my head for the past 10 years were rushing to the front. All I could think was, "Where do I start? How can I do this?"

I was clearly overwhelmed by what had just happened to me. But I took a deep breath, sat down, and thought, "Okay, first things first. I'll do the calendar." The calendar is the schedule; it lets everyone know where to be and when and what we're doing. To me, that was a logical starting point. It wasn't taking on the entire job in one fell swoop; it was breaking it down so that I could do something that would point me in the right direction. So I sat there and got the calendar done from January to July, and immediately I felt as if I had some sort of grasp on the situation.

A friend of mine was faced with moving from a house she had lived in for 11 years and had just two months to do so. She kept looking at all the stuff she had accumulated over the years, and she found herself sitting on the couch staring into space, wondering how she was ever going to get everything packed and moved. But she told me she listened to my voice about paring things down and just did one area at a time. She didn't think about the enormousness of the move; she just concentrated on doing a little bit each day. Doing that gave her confidence that the move would get done if she just kept chipping away at what she had to do.

I've also found that if I'm overwhelmed by the things I have to do on a certain day, I make sure I write everything down. You're never as organized in your head as you can be on paper. Seeing it there in front of you makes the task seem not so impossible. It also lessens your chances of forgetting to do something important.

Show Them the Numbers

When you want to make a point, find the facts that support your purpose. They're there; you've just got to dig. In the 2003 season, our team was 6–10. People look at losses; they say, "You lost this many games; bad football team." It certainly wasn't what we wanted to do. But just looking at that stat did nothing to help my guys get back on track. So I searched a little, and I found out that our stats weren't that far off from what they had been the year before when we won the division. Seven of our losses were by 7 points or less. Suddenly we didn't look so awful. The guys said, "Hey, we weren't that bad. This thing is fixable."

Going into the Monday night game that season against the Tennessee Titans, they were 9–2 and we were 4–7. I said, okay, they've won 9 games. But only 3 of those wins came against a winning team. Heck, we beat 3 of the teams they beat. They've got 9 wins; we beat 3 of them. Guess what? They're not that good. The perception says they're solid, but in reality, here's what they are.

And then I broke them down into quarters and said, "Watch how they play. Look how they play in each quarter. They score points in the first and second quarters, but teams are outscoring them in the third and fourth. What that means is that if they get up, they put you in a game you don't want to play. They can rush the passer, blitz you, confuse you, mess up everything you're trying to do. What we have to do is stay close. Don't make it a two-score game. If you can stay within three points, you got it. Stats show that after halftime, they don't want to play the same game. And they're not good at playing the game we're getting ready to play." The game came, and they got a touchdown right away. I said, "Don't worry, it's one score. Don't get down by two now." We got in at halftime up 10–7. I said, "We're up, guys; they don't want to play that game."

What I did was break down the numbers to show them our strengths and the other guy's strengths and weaknesses and to find a formula that would help us win.

It's the same process when you go over a household budget with your wife. You write down the numbers, how much you pay for groceries, utilities, mortgage, car, gas, insurance, whatever it is, and then you find a way to crunch where you can or expand where you have to. It might not seem that you're spending a lot in one area, groceries, for example (you don't have steak and lobster every night), but the numbers don't lie. You're spending way too much, so you look at the numbers and make a plan to eat more beans and rice, or whatever it is that can lower that expenditure. In business, it may not seem like you're spending much on marketing, but once again, you look at the numbers and the numbers don't lie, so you take them and you adjust. It's a simple theory that nobody can dispute.

I like to use facts because you can't argue with facts. Perception may say one thing, but the numbers might say something else.

Exhaust Your Options

This is what you have to do when you've got a goal and you hit what seems to be a big roadblock. You're driving along, and the road ends. What do you do? You find another way. Maybe you have to get out of the car and walk through the forest. You're working on a big project, and your computer crashes. So you get out a pen and some paper. You find another way. In just about everything in life that is threatened by a problem, there is usually another option.

Last spring they changed the code to the security gate in front of the Jets' complex. It's this big, menacing-looking gate that Bill Parcells had installed when he was the head coach. Well, they changed the code, but nobody told the current head coach. So I arrive at camp at 4 a.m., like I do every single day of the year, because that's my time to work out, to reflect, to get ready for the day. It's important to me. It sets my mind for the next 12 hours, and it's something that I've done as long as I can remember. So I'm sitting there in my car thinking that the gate will open and I'll drive through and park as usual and go get that workout in. I'm pushing buttons and pushing them again, expecting the gate to slide open. But it doesn't. So I try again. It still won't move. Hmmm, I think, "Did they fire me already? They didn't even let me get to the season yet."

So I start thinking, "How am I going to get inside to get this workout in? I've got to get it in, because if I don't, my day starts out wrong." So I look up at the top of the gate, and I figure I'll just climb over it. So I go park my car and then I climb the fence.

I was so miffed, I told my players I was boycotting the parking lot for the rest of the season. The bottom line was, I got the workout in, and my day was saved. I found another option. One of my guys said later that Parcells would have found another option, too: drive through the fence.

The same thing happened when I was supposed to meet the commissioner at the combines in Indianapolis after the 2002 season. The commissioner had called and wanted me and some other coaches to come a day early to meet with him. The day before the meeting, it was snowing like crazy in the New York area. Flights were delayed or cancelled, and I said, "You gotta be kidding me." The commissioner wanted me there. I'd told him I'd be there. So I grabbed one of our scouts and said, "Let's go." "Where are we going, coach?" he asked. I said, "We're driving." We drove 13 straight hours to get there. I said, "I've got to find a way to get there. I told the commissioner I'd be there, so I've got to see what options I have to do that." To me it was simple. I said, "We're driving," and they said, "What?" and I said, "We're driving. Let's go." I got there, and the commissioner was shocked. But I'd told him I'd be there, and I found an option that would get me there.

Most often, there is another way. It's getting people to think like that that is the challenge. Your daughter goes out with a bunch of kids. You've given her an 11:30 p.m. curfew. But they're a ways from home, and the group decides it wants to go someplace even further away from home. Not wanting to drag the group down and make them take her home, your daughter goes along, breaks her curfew, and scares you half to death.

"I had to go with them; I had no choice," she pleads.

But actually, she had several choices. She could have called you to come pick her up, or she could have called another friend; she could even have called a taxi. She had options available to her; she just didn't think about them.

There is always a different way of thinking about something, and there is usually a different way to do something. If you can get that lesson across to your daughter, or your employees, or your players, then you've given them a tool for making good decisions. If your daughter had considered other options, she wouldn't have scared you, and she wouldn't have had to spend the next three weekends at home because she broke your rules.

Do the Corners

When I got to be about eight years old, I asked my dad if I could make some money by raking the back yard. He said yes, and so I went out and I raked hard, working hard. I got all the dirt and the leaves piled up, and I called to my dad because I was ready to get paid. My dad came out and said,

"Son, did you do a good job?" I said, "Oh, yeah, dad. I did a good job." He said, "Really?" I said, "Oh yeah, dad. I did a good job."

He walked over to the corner of the yard and he said, "Son, there's some leaves still here." Then he walked to another corner and said, "You've still got some here, too." And then he walked back to where I was standing and he said, "Son, you didn't do the corners."

I protested, "Dad . . ."

He said, "Son, you didn't do the corners. That's the most important thing in life. Do the corners."

It's a lesson I've never forgotten. Too many times we forget about the importance of taking care of details. We paint a canvas with a broad brush, but we forget to use the small brush for the little things that make all the difference in the painting. When we look at a door, we see only the door; we don't see the hinges, which are what make the door go back and forth. Without the hinges, the door stays shut. We see only the door and forget about the hinges. And suddenly the door doesn't work, and nobody can figure out why.

Do the corners also means don't cut corners. Basketball coaches who know this make sure their players touch the line when they're running gassers; soccer coaches who know it make sure their players don't take shortcuts when they're running laps around the field.

It's the same thing in life.

You don't write a report for your boss without first researching every little fact and making sure everything is absolutely perfect before you turn it in. Because if you don't do this, if you don't pay attention to detail or you've saved yourself a few steps by not looking something up or making that extra call, then you can rest assured something's going to be wrong. A fact here or there, a miscalculation—something minor is going to derail that entire report and all of your efforts. All because you cut corners.

Life is a step-by-step process. You take one step and then another. You don't skip over a step because it's time-consuming or boring or too difficult. You just take the step. If you're teaching a child to read, you don't just hand her a book. You teach her the alphabet, then phonetics and how to sound out words, and then how to recognize certain words. If you skip any of those steps, that child won't be reading any time soon.

Often it's the littlest things that mean the most. You leave a note for your wife saying goodnight when she comes in late and you're already asleep. You mention to your daughter that she has a great collarbone when she's trying on dresses. You call your mom out of the blue just to chat. What you think are little things are often big things to those on the receiving end.

And often it's the littlest things that bring you the most gain. You triple-check a valve on a heating unit, and on the last check, you find that there is a spring missing that could have caused a fire. You take an extra reading of a voltage meter to be sure the equipment is running properly, and you find that the voltage is dangerously high. Nobody asked you to take that extra reading, but you did it because you knew how important the voltage level was if the equipment was going to run safely. You paid attention to detail. You did the corners.

Sometimes we become so complacent, however, or so content, that we forget the corners we did in the past to get to where we are.

Say you're in a great relationship with a great person and everything's going along just fine. Somewhere down the line, though, you stop talking to that person—I mean really talking, about issues and ideas and situations and theories, the kind of conversation that made you fall for each other in the first place. You're talking, sure, but the conversation is stilted. It's about what you did that day, or what you're going to do, or what you want to do, or it's only about the problems that you face each day with work or the kids. And even worse, you've fallen into a pattern. Gone is the stimulating dialogue, the exchange of ideas and dreams and anything with depth. You're going along fine in this great relationship, and you know you've got this great person, but something isn't quite right. You search and search until you realize it's the details, the smallest things that you've forgotten about—intriguing conversation sparked by meaningful questions. Once you realize what the problem is, it's usually easy to fix. When you're facing a problem you can't quite get a handle on, break it down to its smallest parts. That's usually where you'll find your answer.

Football players who don't get in the weight room when they're supposed to or run sprints when they're supposed to find themselves in a bad situation fast. Many of the guys at the pro level believe that they've already got it made because they've been successful. But once they start cutting those corners that got them there, they find they're out of football as fast as they made it in.

In the 2002 season, when we went from worst to first, it was taking care of details that got us there. We started out 2–5, but once we started doing the corners, working every single day on footwork, tackling, and blocking, we started finding success. We didn't leave one corner undone. We got 8 wins in our next 10 games and won the AFC East Divisional Championship.

Ask Tough Questions of Yourself

To be successful, to accomplish your goals, you've sometimes got to be hard on yourself. You need to take a good look inside and say, "Where do I need to improve, and how do I do it? What do I need to do to become better?"

Sometimes it's how to become a better parent, a better friend, or a better employee. Sometimes it's how to become a better spouse. But there comes a time in all of our lives that we need to examine ourselves and ask if what we're doing at something is our best.

I challenge my players all the time to ask themselves and challenge themselves to figure out what they can do better as a player. I ask my coaches that, too. And I ask it of myself every day. I begin my day by trying to figure out what I did yesterday that I need to fix today. I know that if I push everyone around me, I need to push myself, too.

A team player . . .

Visualizes what can be.

Understands the big picture.

Realizes that his freedom to do his own thing has ended.

Knows that his obligation and responsibility to the team come first.

Has a commitment to goals.

Trusts his teammates and puts value in the team.

Respects his teammates' individual differences.

Handles conflict successfully.

Communicates openly and freely with his teammates and coaches.

THIRD QUARTER—
FINDING AN EDGE

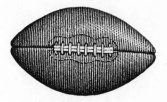

Try not to become a man of success; rather become a man of value.

–ALBERT EINSTEIN

Now you're on the threshold of seizing the game. You're playing great, you've made your adjustments, and now it's time to find something extra to get yourself over the hump. Maybe it's a trick play here or there, or maybe it's just being smarter than the other guy. Sometimes it's not letting problems overwhelm you by—being proactive and remembering what has made you successful so far. The third quarter is important in that you're gathering everything you can for that final push to victory.

When You See Opportunity, Seize It

I think my greatest accomplishment in football was making the Eagles my first year as a free agent. I ended up starting for 10 years, and I never missed a game or a practice. I showed up at work every day, and everything else came about as a result of that. Nobody took a chance on drafting me, but I got my foot in the door through free agency, and I wasn't about to let that door shut in my face. I seized the opportunity that was given to me.

You never really know when opportunity is going to present itself. So you've got to be prepared when it arrives. The Eagles took a chance on signing me, and I wasn't going to let anything keep me from reaching my goal of making that team. I worked out harder than ever before; I studied game film; I spoke with other players on that team. I arrived at camp in the best shape I'd ever been in with the attitude that I would not fail. And I didn't.

If you could look at everything that comes up in your life as though you were seeing it for the first time or the last time, you would be very excited about that opportunity. That's how I look at every day when I head into work: I think about it as my first day of coaching. It could well be my last, too. I'm fully aware of that. But because I never know what's going to happen, it never seems routine. I know I need to take advantage of whatever opportunity arises during the day, even if it's something as small as a chance to have a conversation with a player I don't know as well as some of the others, or to get an extra half-hour of a workout in because a meeting got postponed. Then I have accomplished something by looking at the situation as an opportunity and deciding not to waste it.

It also means recognizing when there is an opportunity that you may not want to take, but that is something you know you should take in order to better yourself and help you accomplish your goals. A young man I know was invited to enroll in a college honors economics program his senior year. Since it was his senior year and he was ready to get on with life, he at first said no. His first three years had gone fairly well—economics had come easy to him, and he wasn't sure he wanted to work that hard. He knew how difficult the program's workload was, especially the final senior thesis. He said he wasn't looking to be challenged until they invited him. Finally, he decided that the challenge would be good; it would be a chance to learn even more about a topic he loved and would put him in a different position in life having an honors economics degree. He took the class, embraced the challenge, and ended up graduating summa cum laude.

He hasn't put the degree to use yet—he ended up going from college to an unpaid internship in the film business. But he's not sorry he took the course. He knows he can always work in that business if he changes his mind, and by taking the course, he learned how to write and he learned that he likes to be challenged. He took advantage of an opportunity that taught him those valuable lessons.

That doesn't mean you should jump at every opportunity that arises. It's important to evaluate an opportunity and decide whether it's something that feels right for you. Before I took the Jets job, I had several opportunities to take coordinator positions with other teams. But these situations, for a variety of reasons, weren't right for me at the time. When the Jets job opened up, I was called for an interview, and I had several other interviews lined up around the league, including Detroit and Houston. I went up to New York first because I had a really good feeling about what was going on with the team. Bill Parcells had set up the team well, and his successor, Al Groh, had decided he was a better fit in the college game and left to coach Virginia. So the Jets were on the hunt. I knew Terry Bradway from my days with the Chiefs, and when he became the GM I started feeling even better about the situation.

They called me in for an interview with Terry and the owner, Woody Johnson. I flew into New York Sunday night, and on Monday, armed with a thick notebook containing my ideas and philosophies about the game, I spent seven hours laying out my plan to lead the Jets to the Super Bowl. When it was over, I was exhausted but exhilarated. I felt as if we had connected. The chemistry was there. The question was, would they take the chance? I flew back to Tampa and told Lia, "I think this thing's going to happen with the Jets. I think I got the job."

Two days after the interview, they called me and offered me the job. I knew the opportunity was right, the timing was right, and besides, they had enough faith in me to offer me the job. Who was I to turn them down? I cancelled all my other interviews, and Lia and I flew to New York to meet the media. I knew it was an opportunity that might not present itself again, and I was jumping in with both feet.

I tell my players that God gives everyone four cards and you can play them any way you want, and, oh yeah, God doesn't deal bad hands. So at the end of the day, if you didn't play them right, it's your fault.

Don't Be Afraid of What You Don't Know

Ignorance is never a defense, but too often we all make judgments based on a belief that we know the truth when it's very clear from the outside that we are afraid of the answer.

My mother was raised in Stuttgart, Germany. My father was a black military man stationed there for a time. They met and fell in love and got married. I don't know if they ever considered the ramifications of a biracial marriage; they figured they were in love, and that was all that mattered. Biracial marriages are very common in the military—when someone is stationed overseas somewhere at a certain age, it's often simply who they meet, who they socialize with, and who they get to know.

My parents weren't treated that great in Germany, and after enduring a two-week-long ride on a Navy tanker to get to the United States, they found out that the Americans weren't real happy with them, either.

They settled in Monmouth, New Jersey, where I was born, and then were moved to Fort ORD Army base in northern California when I was about five. Eventually they bought a small house in Seaside, California, a middle-class city of about 30,000.

My parents chose Seaside because it was closest to the base and more affordable than Monterey's Carmel or Pebble Beach. Their house (a small three-bedroom with a nice yard) cost about $15,000 back then. But it was their first house, and my mom still lives there today. She's comfortable there and has found no reason to leave. We're probably the only original family that still lives on the block. It's nice for her because all my friends know where to go to look in on her and make sure she's okay.

But back in the day when we first moved in, there wasn't a lot of love thrown their way because of their racial makeup. It had to be tough on my mother, who had left her family to come to America to start another life with a man she loved dearly and then found herself in an environment that didn't understand anything about her or my dad. I know it had to hurt when the neighbors gave them the cold shoulder when we first moved in, but she never showed the strain. Mom simply went about her business of making a good home for her husband and their two children and didn't pay attention to the fuss. She knew who she was and what our family was about, and anybody who didn't, well that was their problem.

My parents' approach to the neighborhood ignorance was a great model for me to follow when I finished middle school. The area was in a state of flux because the courts had just ordered desegregation. Monterey High School was in need of some kids of color to come over and integrate the school, and I was one of the many who were chosen to be bused to fill out school board's quotas. Here I was living a couple of miles away from Seaside High, but instead of walking to school, I was spending 20 minutes riding on a bus—each way—to go to Monterey High. The worst part wasn't riding the bus in the morning, it was coming back at night because the Seaside kids were dropped off last, meaning that we were on that bus forever and many nights I didn't get home until 6:30 or so.

Those first few days I felt really anxious about what was going to happen. But my mom, who knew firsthand what I might face, told me to stay strong and stand my ground. She reminded me that with change comes anxiety, but in time everything would be fine.

That gave me great confidence. I knew I was going to be a star athlete, and I embraced that attitude from that first ride on the bus that first day. Kids would ask me how I was going to get home and I told them I had a limo—a 52-passenger limo—and they laughed when they saw me get on that big yellow school bus and wave good-bye. I handled a lot of things with humor and the grace my parents instilled in me. It also helped that I was performing pretty well on the football field—never underestimate the power of being a star athlete.

So many of us like to think we know everything. And then it becomes safe to do only what you know. If you haven't been around black people or Chinese people or Muslims, you really don't know how to act. So you fall back on what seems safe: "They're different; therefore they must be bad." So many people don't ever learn about what they don't know because they're afraid of it, so they allow their lack of knowledge to become so rigid and set that they can't or won't learn anything new.

A perfect example came following the worst day in our nation's history, September 11, 2001—the terrorist attacks on the city of New York and, by association, the American people. We found out that the terrorists were Muslim, from a foreign country, and that they caused the deaths of thousands of people. And because most of us have never been around Muslims, we immediately rushed to judgment against anyone who even looked like a Muslim (not that we really knew what that was, either). I heard so many stories of innocent people being persecuted because of the fear that had gripped the country. Black people know the stories of racial profiling only too well, and now we're adding Muslims or Arabs or anyone who looks Middle Eastern to that world. Nobody knew any better. Many people were afraid even to get on the same elevator with a guy in a turban or a woman in a long robe. It took education to get people to stop being afraid of what they didn't know. That's not to say that the problem has been completely solved. But I do believe that the country has done a pretty good job of realizing that many Muslims are Americans, too, and felt the pain of the terrorist attacks just as greatly, if not even more so because of their religion, as everyone else did.

The same thing happened when Magic Johnson announced he had HIV, the virus that can lead to AIDS. The country panicked. If someone like Magic Johnson can get this deadly disease, what does that mean for the rest of us? The ignorance was amazing. Karl Malone, who played for the Utah Jazz then, came out and said he didn't want to play against Magic, who made a comeback a few years after the announcement, and he wasn't afraid to step up and say so. He was afraid he'd brush up against Magic and get

HIV. He didn't know any differently, and he voiced what a lot of other NBA players were feeling, but weren't bold enough to say out loud. Eventually, though, through Magic's foundation and an increased awareness of how the disease is transmitted, people learned. They found out that it isn't transmitted by brushing up against someone, or sharing a table, or sitting next to someone on a crowded bus. Gradually, the American public began to learn, and today the awareness of HIV and AIDS has never been higher. A lot of people credit Magic for educating the public not only about the disease, but about how to prevent it in their own lives.

Sports, in many ways, are a great teacher. The NFL wouldn't exist without a diversity of backgrounds. Neither would the NBA or Major League Baseball or the National Hockey League. In each, we have a mixture of cultures, and when you put different cultures together, we have learned, you become smarter as an organization. Diversity training in large companies isn't to fill quotas anymore. Smart managers know that there is strength in pulling together different people from different backgrounds and allowing them to work out solutions to problems, create new ideas, formulate new and different ways of looking at situations.

Our team is like that. We have guys from all walks of life with different stories and theories and ideas, and they're all focused on one goal—winning. They've learned about one another, and they've learned from one another. They know each other now and realize there was never anything to fear.

Knowledge is empowering.

Know Your Opponent, but Don't Dwell on Him

My dad always said, "Don't worry about the garbage in your neighbor's yard. Worry about the garbage in your own yard." Obsessing with whom you're trying to beat, whom you're competing with, is easy to do, in football and in life, but it's counterproductive. If you focus so much on what that other guy is doing well, you fall into the trap of forgetting what you do well. All of a sudden you don't play to your strengths; the others have already nullified your strengths because you were so concerned with their strengths. So now you're playing to your weaknesses.

In my third season with the Philadelphia Eagles, back in the late 1970s, John Ralston, the former Stanford and Denver Broncos coach, was Dick Vermeil's advance scout. He'd go watch our next opponent play that week and come back and give us an idea of their weaknesses and strengths. One week he had scouted Houston, and he came back and told us, "They've got this guy named Billy (White Shoes) Johnson. If we kick the ball to the left, do not chase him. He will not be coming back." I still remember that and laugh. Obviously, we learned we shouldn't kick the ball to Billy, but it wasn't something we thought about every single minute.

We watched a lot of game tapes back in those days, just as we do now. But now, a computer analyzes all that for us. I had a projector at home, and I'd chart my opponent's tendencies in different formations. Sometimes the film was so bad you couldn't even see the number on a player's back. At practice, we'd have film sessions and the tape would break or the projector bulb would burn out and we'd sit around waiting for someone to fix it. I remember walking by the coaches' room and seeing tape strips hanging from the ceiling.

That's when I learned I couldn't worry too much about the team I was going up against (actually, I didn't have much of a choice, but I wasn't all that concerned).

Obsessing about an opponent, however, is an easy trap to fall into. I've seen it happen at a lot of NFL and college teams, where they work so hard on what the other guy is going to do that they forget to put in their own game plan.

Say you're in sales and your competition opens another avenue over here and you get so concerned with that little thing they've got that you lose sight of what you've already accomplished and what you're doing. You start concentrating so much on your competition that, you know what, what you have starts slipping. Before you know it, your strength becomes your weakness. This is not to say you should close your eyes to what that guy is doing. You always have to know, but you can't stay so focused on the other guys that you lose track of what it is you're doing. Don't be dominated by them. Always say, "What are *we* doing to get better?"

I have a friend who is very good at her job at a public relations firm. She had all these top accounts and was taking the city by storm. And then her company went and hired a new employee to work in the same office. My friend panicked. She started wondering whether this new person was going to cut into her action. "What if he starts going after my accounts? What if they ask him to do more than me? What if he's there just to push me out? How worried should I be about him?" When she called me one day, she started laying all this out to me, and I stopped her and asked, "How much time do you think you've given to worrying about this guy?" She answered, "Weeks. It's all I can think about. It's driving me insane. Every move he makes, I'm wondering why he's doing it, what's his motivation. Everything."

I asked, "Gotten any new accounts lately? Increased your communication with the ones you have? Done anything to strengthen your hold on what you've got?"

"Not much," she said.

She had wasted so much energy thinking about what this new guy was doing that she had forgotten to pay attention to what she was doing. She had lost sight of what she had done to get herself to where she was. All she needed to know was that there was a new guy in the office and then go back to working on what had made her successful in the first place. You can't control what that new guy does; you can only control what you do. What he does isn't important. You know him, you know his name, you say hello in the office. You might even have coffee one day. But you can't make that new guy your focus. That will lead you straight into trouble.

I can't beat the Giants if I know only their game plan. I've got to work on my own.

You Can Treat People Differently as Long as You Treat Them Fairly

"Isn't that a contradiction?" you ask. Not to me. And here's why. For me to treat one of our top players the same as the fifty-third guy on the roster wouldn't be right. That top player has probably accomplished a lot in the league, and he has earned the right to be treated a little differently. Curtis Martin, our veteran Pro Bowl running back, deserves to have a different set of rules because he has proven himself over and over and over again to be not only a man of great talent, but a man of great integrity. But that last guy on the roster—that fifty-third guy—hasn't proved anything to me yet. He hasn't shown me that he will fight for that extra inch or dive into a pile for a loose ball, and he hasn't shown me that he will stay after practice as long as it takes to get something down cold. Curtis Martin has.

Everyone always says you have to have the same set of rules for everyone on a team. I don't buy into that. I'll treat that last guy on my roster fairly—you can take that to the bank—but he's going to have a different set of rules and standards from my top player.

Say I'm not a football coach, I'm a bank manager. I've got to leave the bank early one day, and I've got to find someone else to lock up. I'm going to select the guy I know best, a proven teller who has saved my bacon on more than one occasion. That's the guy I'm going to hand the keys to the vault to and ask to lock it up. I'm not picking the first-week trainee. I'm not picking some guy who just transferred from another branch. They're all tellers, and they're all held accountable to certain rules and regulations, but the guy I'm going to trust is the guy who has already proven himself to me. That's not unfair to the other guys; it's a responsibility that the guy you know and trust deserves.

One of the great phrases in life that puzzles the heck out of me is the excuse people give when they don't want to do something for you. They say, "Well, if I do it for you, then I have to do it for everyone else." I always say, "No, you don't."

Now maybe if you're a little kid handing out gum to the other kids, this wouldn't apply. But just because someone does something for you or allows you to do something different or special doesn't mean that person has to do it for everyone else.

If I give a kid five dollars, that doesn't mean I have to give all of his friends five dollars, too. Maybe I know the kid and I know he doesn't have any money and I know he needs the five dollars because he hasn't had anything to eat all day. That doesn't mean I'm being unfair to the other kids; I'm just treating him differently.

I know a guy who was so hung up on treating his four sons exactly the same that if he gave one son $100, he would mail checks to the other three on the same day. When the kids were growing up, at Christmas, each son would receive exactly the same number of presents worth exactly the same amount of money. Their dad wanted to be fair and equal.

And further down the road, after the boys had grown up and developed their own careers and lives, their dad still gave to the others what he gave to one, not wanting to seem as if he was biased or treating anyone unfairly.

What he didn't take into consideration, however, was that his sons were not the same. One had become a very rich real estate developer, one had become an orthopedic surgeon, and one had developed a new kind of software for a computer company. Those three were very successful. The fourth, however, had tried a life in sales but had come to learn that his real passion was to open a bakery. So he quit his job and sunk all the money he had earned into this bakery, with the design of opening a catering business. But it wasn't long before he found out how tough it was to make a go of a start-up business. He was having trouble making ends meet. Things got so bad that at one point he called his father and asked for help. And as his father found himself saying, "I can't give you the money because I'll have to give it to your brothers, too, and I don't have that kind of money right now," he realized how foolish that sounded. Obviously, his other three sons didn't need the money; in fact, when he talked to them about it, they said they would have refused it if he had insisted on sending them checks. They convinced him that treating them differently didn't necessarily mean he was treating them unfairly. He gave his fourth son the loan, which was repaid within a year.

Relax, but Be Alert

You cannot allow the pressure of what you're trying to achieve keep you tied up in knots. You have to find a way to relax, to have fun, to enjoy the moment, but stay alert. I don't mean relax and go to sleep. It's relax, but be alert.

The pressure was never greater on our team than in the playoffs in 2001, my first year as head coach. We had just beaten the Raiders on a field goal to end the regular season, and we found out that we had to go back into the black hole for the first round of the playoffs. I could sense the team tightening as it dawned on it that we were going to have to beat the Raiders twice in Oakland in barely two weeks if we were going to stay alive in the race for the Super Bowl. The guys weren't themselves. They seemed nervous and uptight, and this was not a nervous, uptight group.

I knew I had to do something. So after practice the day before we were to leave, I announced that on the charter flight, we would be holding a best-looking sweat suit contest, the winner of which would get $100 directly from my very own pocket. I could feel the mood start to lighten. The thought of taking money from the coach who issued fines for almost anything was too much for my guys.

So on Friday morning we're getting on the bus getting ready to go to the airport and here comes our quarterback,

Vinny Testaverde, in one of the ugliest velour getups that I had ever seen. I mean, it was bad. It must have cost him $250 at one of those really bad stores somewhere I'm sure I've never been to. And then I look at his feet and he's got the Jordans shoes that match. When he walks onto the bus, we are all falling down laughing. We find out later that he spent hours at the mall trying to find the perfect outfit. We get to the hotel in Oakland, and I announce third place, second place, and then, as everyone's cheering, I announce Vinny as the winner. "Who else?" I ask. He says, "Give me that money, bro."

Even though we ended up losing the game, the tactic worked. I needed those guys to loosen up. Instilling a little fun was the perfect way to do it, and having the quarterback buy into it the most was big-time. It didn't mean we lost focus on what we were going to do; what it did was break through the tension and the pressure and let us appreciate where we were and the opportunity we had earned.

I had told them at the beginning of my reign in New York that we were going to do things a little differently. I said, "Guys, one thing you're going to learn about me is, this is how I feel, this is what I do. We're going to be relaxed, but alert. We're going to have fun, go practice, and play. We're going to do both to the best of our ability, but we're going to be relaxed. That's how we're going to call it. That's when we're at our best."

At first, they thought I was crazy. I kept hearing, "This coach is crazy." But you have to keep in mind that these guys were used to doing things differently. This way was my way. Pressure breeds pressure unless you find some way to crack through it. The sweat suit contest was my way. I just believe that people are at their best when they are relaxed and forging ahead at the same time.

A relaxed and alert teacher with a classroom of unruly kids finds a way to bring calmness to the room. That doesn't mean that she doesn't see the kid in the back who's shooting rubber bands at another kid, nor does it mean that she's lost sight of the lesson she's teaching. It means that she disciplines the rubber-band guy, teaches the lesson, and passes her demeanor on to her students.

It's always important to know what's going on around you, but it's just as important not to let pressure, tension, and stress interfere with what you see. Even in marriage, you have to be careful not to let things at work affect the way you deal with your spouse. And you have to be very alert to how your wife or husband is doing—you don't want problems to fester, and you don't want to be surprised by them, either. Relaxing your mind, your body, your attitude allows you to more clearly see a path to success. It's the people who panic, who are overcome by outside issues, who can't find their way.

I do know that if Vinny hadn't come on that bus looking like a really bad lounge singer, we wouldn't have cut through the tension everyone was feeling, and we would have gone into that situation scared and timid. Actually, I remember thinking at the time that velour never looked so good.

Surround Yourself with Good People

Stick to what you know, and find out what you don't know by surrounding yourself with people who have answers. Find good people who complement what you're doing and then let them teach you and others what they know. I'm not smart enough to think I know everything, but I am smart enough to ask questions when I don't know the answer. And as head coach of the Jets, I'm fortunate that there are guys I can trust to give me smart answers.

I count on my staff, my assistant coaches, every day. They are the people I've surrounded myself with, and they have my complete trust that they'll carry on the message of what we're trying to do, and also bring their knowledge and wisdom to me. I don't have enough time in the day to run into every meeting of every assistant coach and find out what they are saying. I trust my assistants to do what they're supposed to do because I know they're good men. I hired them, and I think I'm a pretty good judge of character.

I also hired them because each of them brings a special dimension to our team. One guy is great at breaking down film; another is great at analyzing play schemes. They give me input all the time so that I can make the best possible decisions as a head coach.

Trusting the people around you is key. When you trust your assistants, it's easy to give them the power to do what they do best. When you trust your secretary, you know that what you ask her to do will get done. I don't sit out there on the practice field wondering if she's going to do it. If I asked her to do it, I know she will.

I think that when people worry about the people around them, it's a sign of pure paranoia. You've got to hire people you can depend on and know that you can expect them to do a good job.

Now, finding those people isn't always easy. When I got the job with the Jets, I was bombarded with calls from guys wanting jobs. We had so many phone calls, at the office and at home. Knowing that each guy calling had just been fired, I made sure I took every call. And when I couldn't take the call, my wife, Lia, took it and wrote down the message, and then I returned the call. That was me respecting them, and getting that message across is very important in finding out who you want to surround yourself with. Besides, some day that could be me. It's the nature of the business. I listened to these guys and I interviewed some of them and I scoured the country looking for the best possible assistants who believed in what I believed in and would help this team accomplish its goal of winning football games.

It's not that hard to see that the best leaders and the best businessmen, along with the best coaches, find good people that they count on to work for them. Trial lawyers find the best investigators because they can't go out and investigate every little thing. They find the people who can and trust them when they go to trial. Their success depends on it.

If you're building a house, naturally you want the best architect, the best electricians, the best plumbers. You don't want the house to fall apart or the wiring to go haywire, so you hire the best. If you're having heart surgery, you want the best surgeon, the guy who has done that kind of surgery many times with many successes.

Now, finding the best doesn't necessarily mean finding the most expensive. Do your own investigating. Don't rely only on someone's reputation or even a referral from someone you know when deciding who is the best—what's more important is finding the best for you. It's easy to pick the top people out of a book, but how do you know they're the best people for you unless you investigate? Just because someone says a certain guy is the best at something doesn't necessarily mean he will work for you. Some of my best assistants have been guys that nobody really has known about, guys that I've come across in my career who made an impact on me one way or another.

It does bother me at times to see how the same head coaches keep getting the open head-coaching jobs. It's as if nobody wants to take a chance on someone who hasn't already had a chance. The aggressive GMs, I've found, are the ones who interview widely and not just from the usual suspect list. The successful teams are the ones that go out and do their own research and find out who else there is out there who might work best in the job.

Now, sometimes that means hiring a guy who has been given a bunch of chances but has been overlooked because, for whatever reason, the perception is that he's been given his shot and he's done. Jerry West, one of the best NBA players and general managers in history, went to Memphis and hired Hubie Brown, who most people thought was out to pasture—he had a TV job, they thought; what did he know about today's kids? All Brown did was get the Grizzlies from a horrible place into the playoffs. Isiah Thomas hired Lenny Wilkens, one of the few to be inducted into the Basketball Hall of Fame as a player and a coach, but someone who most people thought was past his prime—and they started a turn-around. I think a lot about Art Shell, who became one of the first black head coaches in the NFL when Al Davis hired him to coach the Raiders. Davis ultimately fired Shell, and he hasn't been able to get another head-coaching shot since.

What's important here is learning to look hard at the field of possible candidates and not to ignore candidates because of someone else's perception. Do your own work and find your own answers as to who can help you and teach you the most.

I was fortunate in that the Jets' owner, Woody Johnson, and the Jets' general manager, Terry Bradway, were willing to risk hiring me, even though I hadn't held a coordinator's job, which seems to be the big stalling point in most careers in collegiate and professional football. Just because a guy hasn't been an offensive or defensive coordinator doesn't mean he's not ready to run the whole show. Just because a guy has designed only two houses doesn't mean he's not the right guy to design yours.

Sometimes finding the good people means taking a chance on someone. Even with our players, not all of them came from the top schools in the top conferences. Many of the guys who are drafted come from schools mainstream America has never even heard of. Look at the Middle American Conference. It typically has the most guys drafted every year because we in the scouting department look beyond the top 10 teams in the country. That's why we have scouts and predraft camps and individual workouts—to find guys who slipped through the cracks of major college football, but who might become outstanding professionals. Jerry Rice, a Hall of Fame wide receiver, came from tiny Mississippi Valley State in unheard-of Itta Benna, Mississippi—and now Itta Benna is on the map. Michael Jordan was cut from his high school team. Joe Montana wasn't drafted until the fifth round. But somebody along the way was willing to take a chance on his own idea of potential, not someone else's. That's where you find the best people.

Was there anything Jerry Rice or Joe Montana wouldn't have done for Eddie DeBartolo or Bill Walsh, who gave them their shot? Think Michael Jordan would ever have not given his best for Dean Smith, who signed him at North Carolina? They were good people, and I guarantee that they taught the guys who believed in them a lot about their respective sports, about talent, potential, and, ultimately, accomplishing goals.

If I'm a newly appointed bank president, I'm going to make sure I have all the smartest people, the most productive people around my conference table. And then I'm going to make sure I find the hungriest people, who maybe have been overlooked and have untapped talent and creativity. And I'm going to interchange people all the time, looking for the best way to achieve our goals. It's hard to keep changing personnel, but it's important to the final goal. Never stop looking. Never stop believing in other people, but do your research to find out who will serve your needs best.

And remember, perception isn't reality. I'm from California, but that doesn't mean I'm a laid-back, liberal surfer dude. On some days, you won't see a drop of California in me. On other days, you'll say, "Oh, he's a California guy." But either perception doesn't mean I'm not the guy to help you get you to your goals. Look past the perception to find your best people.

Guard What You Say

Here are a couple of my favorite sayings:

> "Our tongue doesn't affect only our destiny; it can also change the destiny of those we bless or curse."

> "It is a wise person who bridles his urge to blurt out everything on his mind. Even fools are thought to be wise when they keep their mouths shut."

In other words, if you don't have anything good to say, say nothing.

Now, a lot of people back in Seaside would be laughing real hard if you told them these were words I live by now, because back then I didn't do a lot of thinking before I spoke. Fortunately, the guys I was speaking to had a good sense of humor, and, even more fortunately, I was able to back up my mouth on the football field.

I think the best example of this came during my freshman year, when I was just starting at Monterey High School, having been bused across town from Seaside. The first day of football practice, I'm sitting in the back of the gym, and the coach, Dan Albert, who is now the mayor of Monterey, is addressing the team. But I'm in the back talking, yapping, showing off, telling them, "Hey, look, I'm playing varsity. I ain't playing no freshman football now, you hear me? I'm playing varsity, so you'd better get used to it."

Now, mind you, I had not yet met the coach and had no idea of what he thought about whether I was going to play varsity, and these guys in the back of the gym knew that and maybe I knew that, but I was mouthy enough to call it like I wanted it to be called, and they're looking at me and saying, "Man, this boy is crazy."

All of a sudden the coach stops talking and says, "Who's back there talking when I'm talking? What's your name, young man?"

I stand up tall and say, "My name's Herm Edwards, coach. But you can call me Mr. Bob."

And everyone looks at me thinking, "Okay, it's official. This boy is nuts. He done went crazy."

Coach Albert shakes his head in disbelief and says to nobody in particular, "Who is this guy?"

I say, "You can call me Mr. Bob because I like Bob Hayes, and like Bob Hayes, who is a wide receiver for the

Dallas Cowboys, I'm going to be a wide receiver on your varsity team and I'm going to wear No. 22 just like Bob. That's who I am from now on, Mr. Bob."

I thought Coach Albert was going to blow a gasket. Fortunately, I must have been a little bit charming, because everyone laughed and I sat back down. And then, once everyone saw what I could do on a football field, they were all calling me Mr. Bob—and that was even after I switched to defensive back because I found out Coach Albert didn't believe in the forward pass, either that or he didn't believe in the guy throwing it. I ended up starting on varsity my freshman year, and before I was done, I broke all kinds of school records, including intercepting 22 passes one season. College scouts would come watch and ask about me, and all my teammates would answer, "That's No. 22. That's Mr. Bob."

So if you asked them now about me holding my tongue, you'd get a lot of nonbelievers. What I do, or try to do, all the time is think about what I'm going to say and how the other person is going to perceive it. It's not easy because your mouth works faster than your mind sometimes. Especially when you're angry. Anger makes it easy to say hurtful things. And it's not always possible to take them back. It's never possible to undo the harm you've caused, even if you spend the next six weeks apologizing.

And people who are angry or hurt tend to fire back with anger and hurt. They'll find the most hurtful thing they can possibly say about you because you hurt them first.

Two sisters I know are worlds apart in personality, ambition, style, and outlook, but they couldn't be closer in their hearts. One runs a very successful ad agency, and the other is a stay-at-home mom. Their fights, I'm told, are legendary. And they've done a lot of harm to each other. Each of them knows how to push the buttons that make the other angry and hurt, and it's reached a painful point many times, especially when the sister with the ad agency makes remarks about the other sister's children and what she perceives as a lack of discipline. Then it's a chain reaction. The stay-at-home sister fires back, "Well, you weren't around for the crying years because you were always working." Which causes the ad-agency sister to say, "Yeah, but at least I have money to take my child on vacation." The cycle gets worse and worse as each tries to "win" the argument. But who really wins? Maybe what one says to the other will be so painful that she can't get over it. Maybe it will hit so hard home that it damages their relationship. It's easy to see how it could.

Before you say something to someone, no matter what the reason, no matter what the emotion you may be feeling, it's important to think, "What do I want to accomplish here? Do I want to hurt her back and 'win' the argument, or do I want to get back to the place we were before the argument began, when we were having fun and hanging out?"

I've said things to people even recently that I've instantly regretted, or realized later in the night were things I shouldn't have said. We all make mistakes that way, and the important thing to do when you do say something you believe was wrong is to remedy the situation as quickly as possible. I make a mental note that first thing tomorrow I'm going into that guy's office to apologize for the way what I said came across, that it wasn't the right thing to say and it wasn't what I meant. But whenever possible, I'm a step ahead, wondering how to say what I need to say in the best way possible. Communication is a tricky game that is mastered by the best managers, coaches, and even siblings.

Worry About What You Can Control

What you control about what you're doing is your effort, your heart, your preparation. You cannot control what other people think or feel about you or about what you're doing, and you certainly can't dwell on it. In the NFL especially, circumstances come up every single day. I tell my players, "Don't worry about those circumstances, just play. Let me worry about the media and the fans and the talk-radio hosts and the weather and the crowd and the referees; you just get yourself ready to play. You get your mind right, you get your confidence rolling, and you find a way to react the right way to whatever happens. That's all you can do. You can't worry about anything other than that."

Far too often, I find, people get caught up in obsessing over issues that they have absolutely no ability to change one way or another. A guy I know was in one of the top MBA programs in the country, but he spent much of his time worrying that the program wasn't good enough to get him the job he wanted. All day long it would torment him. "What if it's not enough?" he asked. "What if it is," I answered, "but you've spent all your time worrying about it, and now your grades have slipped and that's what's going to cost you?" All he could do to put himself into position to get that job was work as hard as he could every single day to make himself the best student possible. He shouldn't worry about the reputation of the school; that's not something he can change. And most often, when it comes down to it, the person who wins the job is the person who worked the hardest at proving he was capable. That's something he could control.

Every year in camp, as we get close to cut-down day, I tell them, "Don't try to crunch the numbers, thinking,

'There's no way they're keeping me.' Don't do that; just play." That's something I learned the first time I went through cut-down day as a player back in 1977 with the Philadelphia Eagles. I wasn't drafted, so I really wasn't sure if I was going to make the team. In fact, I was scared that I would get so close to my goal and not go all the way. Making matters worse, my roommate, Skip Sharp, was also a defensive back, and he had been drafted in the fifth round, after the Eagles traded away their first four picks. Dick Vermeil was trying to overhaul the team, and even though I thought I had performed pretty well through camp, I had no idea what would happen.

Like every team back then, the Eagles had a guy who was responsible for telling guys to go see the coach when they had been cut. He did it by slipping a note underneath the door of the player who was being sent home, and he did it in the dark silence of 4:30 a.m. I've always gotten up at about 4:30 a.m., and during that first camp I heard a lot of those papers being slipped under doors. You'd be surprised by what you can hear at 4:30 a.m.

Finally, it was the morning of last cuts. I had agonized all night about what my fate would be. I woke up, and I saw that paper being slipped under the door. One of us was going back to reality. I stared at that paper for the longest time, believing I could maybe will my name not to be there. It wasn't that I wanted Skip's name to be there, just for mine not to be there. It was a horrible feeling that I will never forget. Finally, I reached down and turned the paper over. Skip's name was there. I had made the team. He was cut, but he was sleeping so soundly he didn't know about his demise.

Wanting to make sure that a mistake hadn't been made, I got dressed and ran down to our locker room, which was about half a mile away, praying that my name was still over my locker. Thankfully, it was, and my equipment was sitting right under it. It wasn't until then that I really believed I had made it. I had achieved my goal.

Once it was over, I realized how much energy I had wasted worrying about whether I would get cut or not. I had anguished for nights thinking about how I had done that day compared to how someone else had done. It was so agonizing that I knew I never wanted to go through that paper incident again, even though I knew it would be the same every season. I realized that all I could control was how hard I worked, and the rest was something somebody else had control over. So I set myself up to just work as hard as I could every single day. And every day of the final cut-down, I'd walk to the bulletin board on the wall and search for my name as one of those who had made it. When I saw my name on the roster, I always said, "Tricked 'em again."

If you keep yourself concerned with what you can change or alter, then I guarantee that life will become that much easier to navigate. And I've found it's the best way to battle what I believe is one of the most destructive emotions out there: jealousy. Someone else gets a top assignment that you would have liked to have had. Okay, you feel bad. You're jealous. You start hating that guy and trying to figure out why he got the assignment and you didn't. Chances are, he didn't pick himself for it; some boss picked him for whatever reason. It does you no good to spit venom on that guy or the boss. What does that change? Absolutely nothing. What does being jealous of him accomplish, really? Nothing except to make you feel bad.

What you can do, though, is reassess what you have done in your career that maybe wasn't up to speed with what the other guy has done. Have you worked as hard as you can? Have you developed the proper skills and then practiced them enough so that you could do that particular assignment? If you come up with a no answer, then you know what you need to do next. If you come up with a yes answer, then you move on. The choice was out of your control. Maybe you could call the boss up and find out why you weren't chosen, but in the end, if you're satisfied with your effort, then you just move on.

The same goes for relationships. You're involved with a great guy who has admitted to you that he has had a storied past when it comes to involvement with women. He swears to you he's over it; he's into you, and that's where his focus is. But you can't get it out of your mind. You're wondering whether he's still at it, whether he's still playing the dating game. You sit and daydream and obsess, and by the time dinner comes, you're certain he's cheating on you and you're in a rage, even when there's no reason to suspect him, really. How is that a good place to be at?

What you have to tell yourself is that if he is cheating on you, that's something you can't control. If he is, he is, and it will come to the light eventually. You can't do anything about it. You can't go through life with a guy suspecting his every move. It makes you miserable and petty, and that's certainly not who you want to be. So you tell yourself, I'm not going to worry about what he's up to; I'm going to worry about myself and making sure I'm the confident, happy, sexy person that attracted him in the first place. It saves a lot of bad feelings, and it puts the focus back on you and what you do. You can't lose doing that. Even if you find out he was cheating, you're still better off because you didn't drag yourself down to that level with destructive thoughts and feelings. It might hurt, but in the end, you know it's his loss because of who you are.

This is a lesson that really helped me at the end of the 2002 season, when we ended up winning the division. There were so many parts to the puzzle; certain teams had to win and certain teams had to lose, and people were asking me if I was rooting for certain scenarios. I told them that as soon as you start rooting for teams, it never works. You can't control what happens anyway, and you sit there and waste energy, and it just doesn't work. I just kept preparing our team and our staff and waited to see what happened.

(By the way, we don't use the paper process to let guys go in New York. We handle it with a lot more compassion, mainly because I saw how abruptly it was handled in Philadelphia. We have our position coaches tell the players individually, and each of them knows that I'm available if they want to speak with me. It used to be that the head coach was nowhere around.)

Don't Let the Quicksand Suck You Under

When something bad happens in a football game, most players spend too much time trying to figure out what happened, and then all of a sudden they make another mistake or two and a quarter goes by and the bad guys score another TD and we're down by 14. And then they start to press, and when you press, it makes things worse. You press, and things keep going bad, and you get more frustrated because you start thinking about the situation you're in. And then we're in more than a battle to win the game. We're so far behind that we're trying to catch up. And when you're trying to catch up, it puts even more pressure on you by causing you to do things you really shouldn't be trying to do.

Nobody's quitting, but the frustration is killing them. All they can think about is the missed tackles, the mistakes, and the muck I call quicksand. It keeps pulling you under, and the harder you struggle, the more you get sucked under because you haven't adjusted your thinking. All you can think about is what went wrong, and you start questioning everything you do.

I try to teach my players that when something bad happens in a game, let it go right then. Don't try to analyze what happened, don't try to think through it, don't even think about it one second more. There's plenty of time for all that after the game. But for the moment, while they're in the moment, they've got to think about the next play—what they're going to do, not what they did. That keeps their focus on the task at hand and keeps them from getting cautious, being afraid to make a mistake. Because when you're cautious, you really don't have the ability to make any plays. And at the end of the day, you've given up a ton of yards and a ton of plays because something happened to you early in the football game that got you back on your heels. There are going to be times when you're going to play a little soft, but I don't want our guys playing cautious because that sinks you into that quicksand in a hurry. When you're cautious, you never have the ability to make the big play. You never play the football, and when things are going badly, that's what you need the most.

Often it's not an easy adjustment to teach. Anybody's natural reaction to making a mistake is to panic a little. You put on a bathing suit, for example, and you look in the mirror and you don't like what you see. In fact, you're really unhappy with how bad you look in that bathing suit. "I'm pathetic. I'm fat. I'm a disgusting fat person," is what you say. And you panic. And then that's all you can focus on, and then you get sucked under. You abandon your diet completely because you think it hasn't been working and there is no hope. You grab the ice cream, the cake, the chips and soda, and before you know it, you are being sucked into the quicksand and you're not climbing out anytime soon.

But it doesn't have to be that way. You don't have to go on a fast spiral into the abyss. Just because you don't like what you see doesn't mean you have to get sucked under. What you do is take note of yourself, but quit focusing on what didn't work. You say, "Well, I still don't look like I want to look. I'm still upset by the way I look in this bathing suit. But I've been working pretty hard, and I know I would look worse if I hadn't been trying hard, so I'm going to keep going." You let the moment go and focus on the next thing you need to do, which is to keep from going to the fridge. You changed your thoughts, you dismissed the thing that threatened you most, and you avoided the quicksand.

Getting sucked under is easy with work, too. If I don't take care of problems the day they come up, or at least by the next day, then I know they're mounting up to a point where either I'm going to explode and say something I regret, or I'm going to be so overwhelmed that nothing gets taken care of.

Sometimes this means being really proactive. Say there's a stack of papers on your desk that you haven't gotten to, and it's already 7 p.m. and your family's waiting and your first instinct is, "I'm leaving this. I have no shot at getting these papers done. I'm throwing in the towel. The project is doomed." Instead, I'd sort through them, find the most important, get one of them done, and then go home and vow to start up again the next day. That keeps your head above water a little and gives you something to start on the next day.

The quicksand nearly got us as we began the 2003 season. It was our worst start ever. And when that happens, the room for error becomes much greater. The anxiety level becomes, "Oh, no, we can't lose another one." I was afraid my guys would keep thinking about the bad start, the losses, and consider what we had ahead to be impending doom. My job was to keep them from panicking, and it was hard, really hard.

I'm the head guy, and I see all these other teams with bad starts where it becomes total chaos. And here, with the Jets, we're in the fishbowl of all fishbowls. So I'm trying to hold my guys' hands, doing a lot of reaching out, trying to make them understand why we're doing what we're doing. I've got to get them to focus on the process at hand instead of the process that happened. I told them, "This is when you find out if you really enjoy what we're doing right now. This is when you're playing for that other guy, that guy next to you."

I got them to think about practicing hard each day we practiced. We weren't going to cut anything short; we weren't taking a day off. I wasn't letting them retire after five games, even though we were 1 and 4. I was not about to let them quit; I was making them finish the thing out. To some guys, I said, "You're going to be miserable just like us. I'm not going to pay you to go home now, five games into the season."

Fourth Quarter—
Sealing the Deal

Our greatest obstacles in life are created by people who try to put limitations on us.

–Unknown

We hear so much today about how someone can't finish. A soccer team has forwards who "can't finish," a student spends two weeks writing a report but then "can't finish," someone losing weight can't get rid of that extra five pounds, so she "can't finish." Wrapping things up, sealing the deal, and finishing the project are not easy things to do. It takes a special effort, special heart, and desire to get through those last few minutes or days to reach your goal. Good teams and good leaders learn how to finish; it is an acquired skill driven by a true passion to succeed.

Understand that Winning Matters

Sure it's how you play the game, but winning the game is a heck of a lot nicer than losing. Winning gives you energy. Winning on Sunday makes coming into the office Monday morning something you can't do fast enough. You want to look at the tape; you want to see your guys. They're there early, too, lifting weights, working out. You can see they're walking a little lighter on their toes. Winning makes everything better. You've got joy in your heart; you've got some pride again. You go to the restaurant, and you don't ask for the takeout anymore or sit in the back. The meal tastes a little bit better; your wife all of a sudden becomes better looking. You pet the dog rather than trying to kick the dog. Once you get a taste of winning—at anything—nothing else will do.

Sometimes It's All About the Fighting

There are times when you've simply got to fight. If you've got to kick, then kick. If you've got to scratch, then scratch. Scream, bite—however you do it best, go and do it. Bad, good, or indifferent, if someone knocks you down, get back up and keep fighting. I've heard it said before, if you can't solve a problem, then you're playing by the rules.

That's not to say you should go through life breaking rules. But sometimes fighting a rule for the right reason is an effective way of achieving your goal. I hear about people every day who challenge the system by writing letters, making phone calls, enlisting the help of someone in a powerful position. Sometimes it's what you've got to do.

This goes even for little things, like a restaurant saying you have to wait 50 minutes for your table when you've had a reservation for weeks. You're there at the time you made the reservation for, you're on time, you're ready to eat some good food, but now they're telling you they're backed up and you're going to have to wait. I understand a little bit of a wait, certainly, but unless there was a big kitchen fire or something and they had to run out to buy more food, waiting for an hour is, to me, unacceptable. So you say, "That's unacceptable to us, because we played by the rules. We made a reservation, we showed up here in good faith that we would be able to sit down around the time you said you'd have a table, and we expected that you'd act in good faith, too." Sometimes it works—they find a place for you right away. Sometimes it doesn't, and then you have to judge whether the battle is big enough to take it to the next level by asking for the manager or the owner or calling the Health Department from their phone.

The point is, you don't have to accept something if it doesn't seem right to you. I have a friend who dislocated her shoulder when she fell off her bike crossing some railroad tracks. (Evidently she didn't think the sign that said, "walk your bike across the tracks" applied to her, but that's another story for another day.) She had already had one operation on that same shoulder, when she had hurt it playing volleyball years earlier, and now she was going to need another one. She set up an appointment with her primary care physician, who gave her a referral to an orthopedic surgeon who performed the surgery. Well, the surgery didn't work. Eighteen months later her shoulder was still slipping out of its socket, and she finally decided she was going to have to see another surgeon. She spent hours locating the best shoulder surgeon in her area and made an appointment, and he agreed that she was in bad shape. He said she had only a 50-50 chance of ever being able to play any kind of sports again, but that he thought he could help her.

Relieved, she called her insurance company and was told that they would pay only part of the fees he charged because he was considered an "out of network doctor." This was outrageous to her. She'd already had one bungled surgery, and now they were saying, "We aren't going to pay for your guy; you're just going to have to take your chances with one of ours." Well, that wasn't acceptable to her, obviously. So she got on the phone and stayed on the phone for weeks, and sent letters and faxes. She kept getting denial after denial after denial. Finally, she had one last option, and that was to show that the surgeon she wanted was the only one in the area who knew how to perform the procedure she needed. She got letters from him and from other doctors and their staffs and presented it all to the insurance company. They relented and agreed to pay for the entire thing.

Because she fought, and kept fighting even when she got knocked down, she ended up getting the service she probably should have gotten from the insurance company in the first place.

You can't be afraid to challenge something. It is important, though, to pick your battles, because fighting can be exhausting. You've got to make sure it's something worth fighting for.

That's one of the reasons I really admired Muhammad Ali when I was growing up. He was an incredible fighter, in the ring and out of the ring. He took a stand against fighting in the Vietnam War because of his religious convictions, and he was willing to give up his title for those convictions. That told me a lot about Ali the man. He said, "You know what, you can take all this stuff I don't believe in. I'm not going over there." It wasn't whether he was wrong or right. That wasn't the point. It was that he believed and he was fighting for that belief. It wasn't a very popular stand at the time. A lot of people didn't like him for it. They thought he was a Communist. They called him all kinds of hateful names. Look at him now. Guess what? He's one of the greatest faces out there that people want to meet. My dad was in the service, and even he said, "You know what, son? I don't believe in what the guy's doing. But I admire him. He took a stand."

I maybe followed Ali's example a little too literally. I went to the University of California at Berkeley right out of high school. People at Cal are a little different. They have a voice, and they speak out. That's probably why I wanted to go there. I've always been one to speak my mind, whether it's politically correct or not. It's never gotten me in serious trouble, but it has created a few situations.

I started as a freshman, but it became clear real soon that I was going to have problems with my position coach. He was one of those guys who didn't like anybody questioning his authority, and he met his match in me, because while I didn't question his authority, I was always asking why. Why are we doing this? Why are we doing that? How is this going to make me a better player? He didn't like that, and he let me know it, and I said, "Fine; I'm gone." I transferred to Monterey Community College and got my AA degree. And then Cal wanted me back, so they moved the defensive backs coach to another position and I went back. But then the guy who became my position coach left Cal to join the 49ers, and they moved the other guy back. One more time I said, "I'm gone." I wasn't rebelling; I was fighting my battle. I ended up at San Diego State and had a great year, and we finished 10–1. That was worth fighting for.

It's important to choose your battles wisely. You'll be far more effective in winning those that are truly important to you.

During the 2002 season, after we lost to New England 44–7, I knew I had to get my guys to fight. Simply fight. Get knocked down and get back up fighting harder. I walked into the meeting room and slammed my fist on the projector. That set the tone.

"Gentlemen, this ain't about football anymore," I said. "This is about a fight. We've got to fight to get this thing right."

Eventually we did.

Play to Win the Game

During my second year with the Jets, we started out bad. Really bad. We won our first game, but the team looked mighty ugly. And then, believe it or not, it got worse. All I can remember is that we were in Miami and then we were in Jacksonville, and at the end of both games what I recall is how hot it was outside. It seemed like it was 120 degrees on the field—and it was always the same score. I'd look up at the scoreboard, and I'd be thinking, "We lost by 30 again?" It was like that movie Groundhog Day. It was the same game. And suddenly we were 2-and-5.

Everybody was counting us out, except me. I never felt that we were 2-and-5, that we were going to finish 4–12. I know that for teams that are 2–5, that's generally your destiny in this league, but it was never in my thought process.

So we're 2–5 and I go into my weekly Tuesday deal with the media and somebody asks me if I think my team has quit. And I really couldn't believe what I was hearing.

"Quit? What, are you kidding?" I asked.

"Yeah, have your guys quit?" the reporter asked again.

It was as unacceptable a question as I've ever gotten in my entire playing and coaching career. Because to me, in football and in life, quitting is not an option. You have an opportunity in your lifetime to do something well, and you think about quitting? That isn't on my radar screen.

In sports, you don't quit; you retire. Sure, when you lose, people on the outside start assuming you quit. But my teams will never do that. The whole conversation that day really ate at me. It really did. And it showed. It was one of the few times I raised my voice to the media. But this time, I let them have it.

"This is what the greatest thing about sports is: You play to win the game," I said, my voice rising. "Hello? You play to win the game. You don't play to just play it. I don't care if you don't have any wins; you go play to win. When you start telling me it doesn't matter, then retire. Get out, because it matters. You play to win the game."

My angry outburst was replayed and replayed over and over on just about every TV station in New York and on ESPN. It sort of became my mantra. But it's just what I believe.

What happened was short of amazing. We didn't panic. I'm not a panic guy, never have been. I deal with reality, not perception. I kept hearing that our season was over, and I kept telling my team that it wasn't, because it wasn't—we still had 10 games to play. When I spelled it out, our players began trusting the message, trusting the staff, and I guess they started trusting me. We became the first team in NFL history to go from 2–5 to divisional champs. We played to win the game.

I'm very fortunate because I had a lot of adversity in my life, starting as a young guy. I was crazy enough to play football and play cornerback, one of the hardest positions you can play. Your heart is in your throat every play because basically you are standing out there all by yourself. So your whole life you're covering this guy. So suddenly I'm doing that as a head coach; I'm just playing cornerback right now and still trying to cover this guy. I will try to cover this guy until I go to heaven. That's just kind of my motivation. Sometimes you get beat for a touchdown and you lose the game. But you get back up. I just try to do my best every day. That's how I function.

The way I see it, you get only certain chances in life. You can't waste them because society says you've got no chance. You don't give up on a child with learning disabilities because the doctor says he'll never read. You find a way. You find a special teacher, you find special books, you work with him every chance you can. You give him every tool he needs, and you don't stop until he's reading. Now, this doesn't mean that it's always going to work, but how are you going to know unless you try?

You don't give up on a relationship because everybody tells you it's not going to work. Not if you really believe in the relationship. Everyone has problems; everyone has flaws. If we based staying in a relationship on the number of flaws a person has, we'd have no families, no children, no future. You want to win that game, and you find a way to do it. You change the culture; you change the system.

For my wife, Lia, and me, it's date night. That's something we've discovered we really need in order to keep our relationship strong. Every Friday night, no matter what, is our night. Now, you have to realize that I'm up and at the office at 4:30 a.m. just about every morning and I don't get home until past midnight every night. I leave in dark-thirty and I get home in dark-thirty. That's a lot for a wife to put up with; I know that. So I make sure and she makes sure—because she's not just sitting home doing nothing; she's got just about as many activities as me, what with the charity work we do, the Jets women's organization, and dealing with our families—that Friday night is date night. Sometimes we go out to dinner, but with the excitement we've created with our football team, it's sometimes hard to have a quiet dinner and be nice to the three dozen people who come up to congratulate us, and that's something I just can't let go unnoticed. So we've taken to staying home and renting a movie or just talking. It's something we need to win the game of marriage.

She travels with me on all of our road trips because Dick Vermeil told me when I got this job to always take my wife.

"Marriage is hard enough. You need her with you. Make sure she sits with you on the plane, that she's involved with what you're doing. The road is a lonely place. Make sure she's around. You'll see why."

At first the players were surprised to see a woman on the plane. But we changed their culture, and they soon understood what a priority having her around was to me. Having her with me on road trips has allowed me to win the marriage game and a few on the field, too, because I listen to her.

That said, Lia takes the losses much harder than I do. I remember that 2002 season when we lost against Cleveland to make us 2–5 and Lia cried all the way home, she was so upset. But when we got home, it was Lia who said, "You're not getting through to them. You're not talking to them. They don't hear you. You're a great coach. You've got to find a way to get through to them."

She was right. And it was the next day that I went in and gave them the "you play to win" speech. Guys were telling me for a long time what that meant to them. It gave them their pride back, even though the record said they had no right to pride.

Give everything to what you do, the people you love, and what's important to you, and you will not be disappointed. We might not have gone on to win the divisional championship that year, but because we did not quit, because we played to win the game, it wouldn't have mattered.

Profile of a Winning Team

A winning team feeds on itself, not just by
    attracting better talent, but by raising its own
    level of confidence and passion for the team.

A winning team plays to win, not to lose. That is often the difference between success and mediocrity.

A winning team has a winning attitude. Team members believe in themselves and in their teammates.

A winning team keeps improving. Team members know that if they stop improving, their time is finished.

A winning team is made up of players who make their teammates successful. Few people are successful unless a lot of people want them to be.

Battle the Negative

Every day I wake up and I say, "Something good is going to happen today." You can have a lot of frustrations happen to you during the day, but you've got to take something good back with you before you go to bed. That's always been my philosophy. You can't tell me something good didn't happen today. It might be the smallest of things: Your phone didn't ring off the hook, your daughter gave you a hug before she went out, you watched a movie with no commercials—it can be anything, but find something good, something positive to think about before you go to sleep.

Finding the positive isn't always that easy. A friend of mine had a streak of what most of us would call really bad luck. Her daughter, who was a promising dancer, broke her ankle in three places, and her career was threatened. And just after her insurance company told her it wouldn't cover the surgery because she wanted to use a certain specialist, the right front axle on her car broke—right in the middle of traffic—while her daughter, who had just gotten her license, was driving to see a ballet in downtown Pittsburgh.

Just as she was getting ready to say, "I can't catch a break," I stopped her and said, "You know, look at it this way: You're actually very lucky."

"Lucky?" she asked. "What are you talking about? My daughter is hurt, the insurance isn't going to pay, and my car just broke down."

"Well," I said, "that's one way to look at it. I choose to look at it like this. Your daughter was hurt, yes, but you got her the right care quickly. The insurance won't cover the surgeon you're going to use, but you told me he waived his fee because he wants to help her, and so she'll end up getting the best anyway. And as for the car, thank God it happened while she was at a stoplight. A few minutes more and she would have been on the highway, and I cringe to think about what happens when an axle breaks at 65 miles per hour."

She knew I was right, but she didn't know how to find the positive in such a streak of seemingly negative events. There is always a positive to find, but sometimes you've got to search for it.

During our 2003 season, it was a tough search, trust me. We went into the season with such high expectations and hopes, and then, wham, in our third preseason game, our quarterback, Chad Pennington, broke his hand and we lost six games. Six games. Holding everybody together was the toughest thing I've had to do as a coach. I also think it was my best coaching job so far. I had to keep giving my guys hope. You have to create hope for people because when you deny a person hope, when a person thinks in her mind that there is no hope, she gives up. I've seen it.

I had to create hope and find something positive about our season, and it wasn't easy. We got to the Monday night game against Tennessee, and I said, "Hey, guys, they set this schedule last year. They anticipated us being one of the premier teams this season because of what you've done the last two years. This is your Monday night game, this is your deal." We'd had some bad things happen, but those games were gone and they didn't have to transfer to this game. I said, "We've got to come out and play like we're the team they anticipated us being, the team making a playoff run, and by the way, we still are. Anything can happen."

I convinced them that they needed to be the team winning that game on national TV to show people who we are. We had to get people to say, "You know, they've had some tough games. It's been hard for them, but you know what, watch them play."

I spent all week creating that hope for everybody. Our guys were so fired up. I told one reporter on Friday, "We're going to win this game." Guess what? We did.

I believe in the power of positive thinking. If someone asks me if the glass is half full or half empty, I say it doesn't matter; it's still the same amount of water. But I'd choose the half-full line every time. Negative thinking drains the soul; it makes us weak. I will always see the good in whatever situation I'm facing or whatever problem presents itself. Negative thinking breeds negative results.

A guy I know didn't understand this. He was miserable in his own life, and he was intent on bringing misery to those around him, whether he realized it or not. Every day was a down day. And this was a guy who seemingly had it all. He had money, a nice house, a good job, and a daughter who was a great kid. But he could never find the positive in his own life or, especially, in his daughter's. He berated her constantly, whether it was about her schoolwork, her relationships with friends or, above all, her play on the soccer field. He yelled and screamed during the games and then repeated himself in the car on the way home. He didn't understand that he would have gotten much further with his daughter by finding things to praise and encouraging her to keep working hard. He could not see the positive through the fog his brain had created with negative energy. Eventually, she got fed up and stopped seeing him. It is a sad situation that remains unresolved.

Something that has always stayed with me is a column that Anna Quindlen wrote for *Newsday* about a homeless guy who spent most of his time on the boardwalk at Coney Island even in the dead of winter, wrapping himself in newspapers to stay warm. Here was a guy who had no money, no home, no food on a daily basis, no family around, and she asked him why he stayed out on that cold boardwalk. He answered, "Look at the view, young lady. Look at the view." If that guy can find something positive in his situation, I know I can find something positive in mine.

You can always choose the way you look at something. Find the good.

Don't Be Afraid to Fail

The great thing about being successful is that you have no fear of taking risks. What most people don't understand is that if you don't have the fear mechanism in you, you won't be successful. By the fear mechanism, I don't mean being afraid to fail, I mean being afraid of not being successful. There is a world of difference.

When I told the world I was going to be a professional football player, if I had looked at how hard it was going to be, the struggles I'd have to go through, and the sacrifices I'd have to make, I probably would have talked myself out of even trying because I would have been afraid to fail. But to me, the fear of not being successful was more overriding. I didn't even think about how hard it would be; I just did it. I told people what I was going to do, and the fear of not doing it was a real motivator.

I believe that the only true failure in life is not attempting something you want to do. That's when you fail. You look at the hill and you say, "There is no way I can climb that hill. It's icy. I don't have snowshoes. What am I going to do?" What you don't do is look at the top and get overwhelmed. You look at eye level and take one step at a time. And you don't have to put a time limit on it, either. Just keep one foot following the other and you'll get up that hill.

Now if you attempt it and it doesn't work out—you don't make it to the top because it got too dark or something, and you have to turn around—you didn't fail. The only true failure is if you don't make the attempt.

Say you're taking a test and you say, "Oh, man, I'm going to fail this test." How do you know? You haven't taken it yet. The hardest thing to do is to take that first step, answer that first question. Once you do, though, the fear is over. You go skydiving and you stand there looking out of the airplane and you're scared and you're saying, "Oh, gee, I . . ." But once you take that first step, it's over. The fear is gone because you have no chance to go back. You're skydiving.

Say you want to write a book, but you're afraid it won't be good, or it will be too difficult to stay committed and finish it. Being afraid of it will never get it done. Get out a pencil and paper and put some words on the paper. You don't think about how hard it's going to be to get 300 pages written; you don't think about whether it's going to be a best-seller or not; you start writing down words, and then you're moving along, and eventually you're going to get over being afraid of the task. And if you're doing your best every time you sit down to write, then it does you no good to worry about whether what you've written is going to be good. Doing your best at attempting something you've wanted to do is a successful endeavor; whether the rest of the world thinks it's good is irrelevant. You've accomplished a goal because you conquered your fear of doing something a little scary.

Say you want to find someone to share your life with, but you're afraid you'll never find the right person, or you find the right person, but you're afraid it won't work. How do you know unless you try? You've got to walk out that door first and take that first step into a church choir or a cooking club or some kind of charity. You've got to go on out there and see what there is. A lot of people stand and look at what they want to do. They look and look and stare and obsess, but they never take that first step. They're afraid to fail, so they talk themselves out of it. A lot of people are afraid of relationships because they've been hurt in the past and don't want to risk that again. But how does that help you when you have decided you really don't want to be alone through life? It doesn't. Risking heartache is a big step for a lot of people, but you've got to move past that fear and into a mode where you're not afraid, and I believe that taking a step outside that fear is the first step—deciding that it's okay if it happens again.

I see the same fear in athletes who have suffered serious injuries. So many times, when they come back to playing, they're afraid to be the player they were before the injury because of the fear that they could get hurt again. Overcoming that psychological barrier is difficult, whether it be in relationships or injuries. The ones who are successful look at the situation and say, "Okay, so I get hurt again; what does that mean?" Sometimes it means realizing that if you fixed it once, you can fix it again. That's not to say that the fixing process wasn't difficult, but it's a mechanism that is effective. You had surgery and rehab on your knee once, and, looking back, it really wasn't that bad. Your heart was broken, but now you're okay, and maybe that wasn't so bad, either. It's a matter of perception, of getting yourself to a place where not trying something is worse than a problem repeating itself.

It is true that the more challenge you take on, the more you risk. But at some point, you've got to take that first step toward failure in order to face the challenge on the road to becoming successful.

POST-GAME — VICTORY AND LEGACY

Be humble. A lot has been accomplished before you were born.

–UNKNOWN

You've accomplished your goal—you've lost the weight, you've fin-ished the project, you won the game. Now what do you do? Do you revel in your success, or do you find a new goal, a new project, and a new use of your time? I see so many people get caught up in some-thing they've done to the point where they lose out on winning at something else. For me and my team, there's always another game to prepare for, always another season. We don't pat ourselves on the back so much that we lose sight of what has to be done next week to get us to our ultimate goal. Until we reach that, we won't rest. I know I won't. And when we do reach it, then we'll start over and try to do it again.

If You're Looking for Credit for a Job Well Done, Go to the Bank

We are tested by the manner in which we respond to suc-cess and praise. Does it trigger arrogance and pride, or does it cause humility? How someone handles praise and success can tell you much more about that person than how he han-dles criticism. It's a great equalizer.

When you are praised, it really means that you've been noticed. Okay, you've been noticed—now what are you going to do? Either you're going to think you've arrived and let up, or you use that window—and it's not a big or wide window—to do something really great.

I spoke to a group of bankers once who had just been promoted to the next level. I told them that what that meant was that they had been praised and noticed, and now they had a voice. I said, "Everything you say and do now will be looked upon by others as having a certain validity because of the praise that has come your way. How you handle it— what you choose to do with that voice—is up to you."

Success and praise often bring a sense of contentment, which can lead to complacency, and that is guaranteed to harm your chances of future success. It's like exhaling. You've been building, building, building, and then you've succeeded; you've been praised, you're feeling good about yourself, your friends are calling saying, "Great job." And before you know it, you're just lying on the couch basking in the glow rather than using that glow to find even greater success or to succeed at something new.

I'm always amazed at the number of players who think they've earned the right to slack off once they have a Pro Bowl season or capture some record of some kind. Their thinking is, they've made it to the top, they'll just stay at the top, and we all know it doesn't work that way. The success and praise has made them cocky, and once that happens, their reactions become skewed. In the off-season, if you tell a guy who became a star the previous season that he needs to get in the weight room or on that track, his response is, "I know what I'm doing," when before either he was already doing it or he answered, "You're right, coach, I'm starting that today."

The guy who does this has forgotten what it was that made him great. He's been blinded so much by his success that he can't see in front of him. He thinks that because he has become a star, the stardom will stick on its own. If you forget what you did to get to the level where you are praised and considered successful, you have nowhere to go but down. A guy like this had a small window to take his game to an even higher level by showing that he wasn't satisfied with what he had accomplished, which, in turn, would most likely have increased his marketability as well as his performance on the field. And before he knew it, someone will pass him by. One of our rookies will come into camp like he used to be, in fantastic shape and with a hunger to prove himself. Embracing success is the surest way to make sure it doesn't happen again.

Say you get an award for being the top salesperson in your area. There's a big banquet, a big presentation, they give you a plaque and maybe a bonus, and the attention is squarely on you and what you've accomplished. Sure it's good to feel good about what you've done, but if you spend the next three years coasting on those accomplishments, you'll find yourself out of a job. You are only as good as your last accomplishment, and the "what have you done for me lately?" theory definitely applies to most walks of life.

And even if you find you can't work any harder, you can maintain the level you've operated at to get you to where you are. You stay committed to your goals, you embrace the challenge every day, and you find new and creative ways to stay at the top.

If you look at the top companies in the country, you'll see that they have maintained their excellence by doing those things. They've become successful and they've continued to be successful by working hard every day and changing when change is necessary, either with products, advertising, community outreach, or philosophy. They haven't waited for the rest of the industry to catch up with them, they haven't rested on what they've accomplished; they've pushed on in the face of success.

When we won the division in 2002, we had another game to play, so we couldn't afford to sit back and celebrate what we had accomplished. We felt good for a few minutes—you have to do that; it's human nature—and then we turned our attention back to where it had been during the winning stretch toward the end of the regular season. Nobody was basking in anybody's glory; nobody was patting anybody on the back saying, "Good job. Now you can rest." We were still hungry, and we had a lot to accomplish.

We won our next game against Indianapolis and then fell two games short of playing in the Super Bowl, losing to Oakland in the playoffs. We certainly didn't rest on what we had accomplished.

A lot of people think that overcoming adversity is the toughest thing you face in life. I'd argue that often, the toughest thing you face is overcoming the gratification that comes with achievement. It's far easier, I believe, to over-glorify what you've done than to pull yourself up by your bootstraps and get through tough times. Humility is hard to find once someone tells you you're great. And complacency is the anti-success. It is laziness in the spotlight, and after a while, the spotlight fades and it's just laziness. Those who are truly successful handle praise with humility and success with a smile and a willingness not to let that be their only brush with accomplishment.

Value Your Name

Your name is the only thing you have that has real value. Proverbs 22:1 says, "It is better to have a good name than all the riches of the world." This is something my father instilled in me when I was about 11. He told me that of all the things he had given me, the greatest was my name.

He said, "I left you a good name. Whatever you do, don't screw up that name. I don't care what you do, just don't embarrass that name. Don't do something stupid where people are going to go, 'Too bad about that kid.'"

From the day he told me that, I was scared to death of getting in trouble or embarrassing my mom and dad. Things would come up, and I'd say, "No, I can't do that. Don't do that. Don't go down that road." It also helped that my mom told me that if I ever got thrown in jail, I shouldn't even bother calling home because nobody was coming to bail me out!

Doing the name good has stuck with me to this day. Every time I make a decision or get ready to say something, I'm always thinking about what my dad said. How is this going to reflect on my name?

Valuing your name also means valuing your word. If you give someone your word that something will get done, make sure it gets done. Going back on your word or failing to back up what you say will tarnish your name quicker than just about anything else. It can be as little as taking out the trash because you said you'd do it, or as big as saying you will increase profitability this quarter. If you say it, make sure you do it. Get up 10 minutes earlier to get those trash cans outside before the garbage truck comes. Make smarter decisions about expenditures to ensure that profitability will increase even if sales don't. Don't make promises you can't guarantee. Don't make guarantees that you can't absolutely, without a doubt, say will happen. I never guarantee a win; I never guarantee a certain number of wins each season. I never even make predictions because of the uncertainty of results and because they don't really matter anyway. I do guarantee that I will give my best effort to help get us to where we want to be. I give you my word on that. I'll stake my name on that.

Saying and doing the right thing is even tougher now because of the media attention I get as head coach of one of the most storied teams situated in the biggest media market in the country. There is so much pressure on me now. So many people are looking at me. Every time I say something, I know that somebody's going to hear it. And I'm fearful that someone will hear it and say, "Why did he say that? What was he thinking? Is that man crazy?"

My dad died knowing that I had accomplished something that nobody thought I could do and that along the way, I had done the name proud. I think that meant more to him than anything. The older I get, the more pressure I put on myself because I know I've done a pretty good job and I don't want to screw it up.

All Experiences Are Good

Some people look at an experience and say, "I had it bad." I say it wasn't a bad experience unless it happens to you again. If it doesn't happen to you again, then you've learned from your experience, and that's what makes it a good experience.

That's how you grow as a person. Every experience shapes who you are. You can choose to learn from an experience, or you can choose to ignore it and hope it doesn't come back. You have to ask yourself, "Do I really want to go through that mess again?" And if the answer is no, then use that experience to grow. Ask yourself how you would do things differently the next time and who else you can help to make sure they don't go through it, either.

Here's an example: People get pulled over by the police all the time for drunk driving. Everybody knows you shouldn't drink and drive. You know this. You swear every time you hear a story about someone who was so foolish as to drink a bunch of margaritas or mai tais or whatever and then try to drive home. Maybe he hits another car; maybe he kills someone. Maybe he kills himself.

"That's awful," you say. "How can people not know that drinking and driving can be deadly?" You chastise those people; maybe you even join MADD to support the cause. But then one night, you find yourself in a situation where you've had a few drinks and now you're driving home. And you swerve and the police see you swerve, and now you're being pulled over and they're making you stand on one leg and touch your nose and you can't do that. So they handcuff you and take you to the station, and you're fingerprinted and your mug shot is taken, and they throw you into a cell until a judge releases you.

Okay, it's a bad night. It's a horrible night. What you did could have had horrible consequences. Thank God you didn't hit anybody or anything, and your trauma is simply having been held overnight in a rank jail cell with a bunch of other drunk drivers.

You say it's the worst experience of your life, you anguish about it, you cry. You are embarrassed, humiliated, and angry at yourself. But it really is the worst experience of your life only if you do it again, because then you haven't learned a thing. Your anguish and the long night in jail taught you nothing. Only if you never drink another drop of alcohol before getting behind the wheel can you make this into a good experience. And if you can do that, then getting caught in the first place was a good experience. You learned something about how your beliefs didn't match your actions and about the effect alcohol has on your ability to make a good decision. Knowing this can only help you down the road when you make other decisions involving critical issues.

There is a lesson to be learned from every experience you have. You're driving down the road with your daughter and the radio station plays a Beatles song you both love, and you both start singing at the top of your lungs. Bad singing. Screechingly bad singing. But you're smiling and laughing, and you realize how much you enjoy being with your daughter. You realize you haven't been doing enough of that lately, and you vow to do it more. That's a good lesson from a good experience. It's something to build on.

Your son gets a letter from the college he's heading off to attend in the fall, and in it, a student ambassador describes what college life is like at that university. It details how it will be the best experience of his life, and he immediately gets excited about going there next fall. He says he can't wait. Then he hands the letter to you and walks into the kitchen. You read it, you see all the wonderful things that are about to happen to him, all the great experiences that are in front of him, and you begin to cry. What's the lesson? Are you sad because he's leaving? Sure. Are you sad because he's going to be doing all those things and you won't be around to watch? Of course. But if you look at why you're crying long enough, you'll come to understand that your tears are largely because you're just as excited for your son as he is. You're excited that he is going to get that opportunity to do something really special. Examining why something initially feels like a bad experience can ultimately lead to making it good. Crying over a letter can become a good experience that will shape your thinking as he moves toward that big day of leaving home.

Even in football, the bad can become the good. I had a player once who had a hard time holding onto the ball. Fumbling is one of the worst things a running back can do. This player ran hard and fast, but he just couldn't hang on to the ball—even when he wasn't hit. I finally pulled him aside one day and said, "Son, how do you feel when you fumble the ball?"

He says, "Oh, man, coach, I feel terrible. I feel like someone has just punched me in the gut. It's the worst."

"It feels that bad, huh?"

"Oh yeah, coach. It makes me sick. I go home and I don't sleep."

"So don't fumble," I tell him. "Turn fumbling the ball into a good experience by figuring out a way not to fumble. Get it out of your mind, for one thing. Don't sit there and torture yourself all night long, because all that's doing is focusing on how bad you feel. Next time you fumble, forget about it the second after. See what happens."

The kid was a little confused, but I asked him to try it. Next game, sure enough, first quarter, he fumbles the ball. I look over at him and say, "Forget it. Let it go."

He didn't fumble again for six weeks. He turned fumbling into a good experience by adjusting his thought process to eliminate equating fumbling with something bad. Bad things don't have to be the same as a bad experience.

Embrace Giving

We must work hard to make a living, but it is what we give that shapes our lives. My dad spent many, many years in the Army as a master sergeant. When he retired, he worked a little in construction, but mainly he became known as the "fix-it" guy on the street. If the plumbing went wrong, you'd call Ed up and he'd come over and fix your plumbing. If your fence broke down, he'd come by and fix your fence. He was always giving something to somebody. Once I asked him, "Why do you do that?" He said, "That's what you're supposed to do in life. It's about giving. It's not about what you're going to get, it's about what you're going to give back." That's truly his legacy.

Besides my dad, I had a lot of coaches who helped me along the way when I was growing up. When I found a little bit of success, I started repaying that debt. A couple of buddies from Seaside and I formed a charity golf tournament with the idea of raising funds to build a new center for the Boys & Girls Club. And we did it. After that, I started thinking that the center was great and all that, but we really weren't touching kids directly. We had given them walls, but we hadn't really had a chance to inspire them or teach them or help them grow. That's something that had meant so much to me as a kid. A coach would take me aside and teach me something new, or tell me something about how to fix my technique or even about how to get along with the other kids. It helped shape me into who I am today, and I believed it was important to try to do that for other kids from Seaside, too.

So we scrapped the golf tournament and started a football camp that was free to any kid who signed up. I said that for one entire week, I would help coach any kid who signed up and promised to be there and give his all. I enlisted the help of a bunch of former teammates and coaches, and we developed this camp, which now draws close to 500 kids each summer. It's an amazing thing to see. Walking onto the field, if you didn't know better, you'd think it was chaos and a half. But it's a calculated chaos. We divide the kids into teams based on age and ability, and then we coach them and teach them, and they play in a system that leads to the Super Bowl.

You might have figured this out about me by now, but I'm not one of those guys who has a camp and then shows up only for the banquet. No, sir. You'll get tired just watching me run around those fields. Because I'm the guy with the name. I'm the guy they want to see and to be seen by. So I make it my business to move all over the field to see as many kids as I possibly can.

These kids come from all walks of life. Most of them are like I was way back when. Not a lot of money, but a lot of drive. Some have very little direction, but they're there because they want to be. I always say the hardest thing to do is show up. These kids show up every day for a week because they want something. That's something I can appreciate.

At the end of the week, we have them all come for a celebration dinner. I get up and say a few things, we take some pictures, and we invite their parents and everyone in their families to see what the kids have accomplished. And it's all free because of donations and the hard work of some of my closest friends, who believe in giving back just as I do. It's a wonderful thing. My mom comes. My mom's friends come. My wife, Lia, runs the concession stands, but I think we lose money on the candy sales because kids are always coming up and she ends up giving them money to buy things. But that's okay, too. These are needy kids, and the thing they need most is people to believe in them so that they can believe in themselves.

When I got to the Jets, one of the first things I did was start a youth football clinic in Central Park. At first they thought I was crazy. "Central Park?" they said. But I've said it all along: We are a New York team. We should be taking our message to the people of New York. The first clinic we had, we had hundreds of kids show up. I also started a clinic for 250 high school football coaches at Fordham University. I know I have a powerful platform from which to preach, and I'm going to do whatever I can to get the message out.

Lia started the Jets women's organization, which raises money for many charities and is involved in many functions for worthy causes.

Giving back doesn't have to mean some grandiose gesture or something that really involves time and effort, like my camps. Giving back can mean something as easy as tutoring a second grader in reading or donating books to a shelter. It's an important and meaningful way to say that you're happy to be so fortunate in your own life. It keeps you grounded, and it inspires you just the same to know that you've perhaps touched someone else's life in a meaningful way.

Share the Spotlight

Every week we pick an extra two or three captains so that they can go out to the middle of the field for the coin toss. A lot of guys never, throughout their career, are able to go out and be involved in the coin toss. It might not seem like a big deal, but to those guys it is. It's a moment in the spotlight that has proven to be very rewarding to our players.

It's important to make everyone feel like they are part of your success, because you didn't get to where you are by yourself. There has always been someone standing behind you or beside you when you've accomplished something great. It's most often your friends and family, but it could also be your coworkers or your competitors or even people you don't know—like fans, for example. When the spotlight shines on you, make sure it also shines on those who helped you along the way. You will reap much more personal reward if you deflect praise to someone else. If you are truly the one to credit, this will not go unnoticed by those who need to notice. Smart managers know that there is never one person to credit or to blame. They can peel back the layers to give credit where credit is due; it's not your responsibility to show it to them.

It is always disheartening to me to see someone who truly believes that his success came solely because of something he did. This is rarely true. I once saw a young man accept an Emmy award for a story he had done for a national television news show. Traditionally, the producers of the story accept the award on stage because, more often than not, they have done the bulk of the work. But this young man was so sure he was the reason they had won that he bounded up on stage before anyone could stop him and accepted the award himself. Worse yet, he failed to mention the producers, who rightfully deserved to be there. I learned later that the young man had done very little in the creation of the story and had angered a lot of people when he stole the spotlight. He had already become known as a lazy, selfish worker, and his actions that night only reemphasized that image. He was never thought of in a good light after that, and it affected him and his assignments long after that night, whether he knew it or not.

I think about him, and then I think about the young girl I heard about who had worked very hard to make the track team and then worked her way to becoming one of the best freshman runners in the city. She won league titles in the 800 and 1500 and went into the city championships as the favorite. The 1500 was first, and this girl found herself running against one other girl who went out unexpectedly fast and strong. It took the girl almost the entire four laps to pull even, and then she won the sprint at the end. Both girls were exhausted, and yet both were entered in the 800. The young woman I heard about thought hard about the race she had just won and how the girl she had just beaten had been such a great opponent that she really deserved to win a city title, too. So she dropped out of the 800, which the other girl won. Each girl came home with a city championship, and while some people might have thought the girl was being a bad competitor, a lot of people were moved by her heart—instead of maybe coming home with two trophies, she came home with one and let the other girl come home with one, too.

There are many ways to share the spotlight. If you think about it, the most gracious winners at the Academy Awards every year are those who remember the people they should thank, the people they should bring into their spotlight. The most gracious people at work are the ones who make sure everyone gets acknowledged for her part in a successful project or event. Great leaders know that their success is dependent on the efforts of others and never let those efforts go unrewarded or unmentioned.

As a coach, I'm in the spotlight on the sidelines before every game, and I make sure I bring each of my players into it, too, by shaking hands with every one of them before every game. Dick Vermeil did this when I was a player in Philadelphia. When he came up to me to shake my hand, I felt that I had a connection with him. So now I make sure I find every guy and let him know that I am with him. It's like a general going out to talk to his troops to let them know that every man is important.

I remember when I was in Tampa coaching John Lynch, I always used to hug him before he took the field, saying, "I can't play anymore, but take a little bit of me out there."

Shaking each guy's hand puts them in the spotlight with me, and I'm saying, "We have 53 guys on this team, and I need all 53 of you."

Very few people are successful unless a lot of people want them to be. Believe me, I didn't achieve my success by myself. I had great parents, but it goes beyond that. People in the community. People I met along the way. A lot of people share my spotlight because I will never forget them.

Instill Pride

After my first season with the Jets, I finally found time to go to my first New York Yankees game, and I knew immediately why that organization is so successful. You sit in the dugout and those players come by and you shake their hand and talk to them, and you say, "OK, that's why these guys win." When you talk to the coach, when you go into the locker room, when you go to see Mr. Steinbrenner, you know they care about winning. You can just sense that, whatever they do, they're going to try to win. They've instilled a lot of pride in that franchise, and you can tell that's why they are in the World Series just about every year, it seems.

Instilling pride really means creating an environment that your players or your employees feel good about being in. Sometimes that means doing something extra or different from what other companies or teams do, to set yourself apart.

It's something I am trying to do with my team—instill pride that we are New York City's team. We may play in

New Jersey and practice in Hempstead, but last time I checked, we are still the New York Jets.

After the terrorist attacks on September 11, I realized that we needed to do something for the city and become the pride of the city. We won't get our own stadium until at least 2008, so all I could really do was change where we stay the night before the games. The Jets had always stayed in New Jersey, but I moved us to downtown New York City, to the Marriott, right across from where the Twin Towers used to stand. I felt it was a good gesture on our organization's part to stay down there. That was the place I felt we should stay as a tribute to what happened there and so that our players could understand how fortunate we really are. The players felt it immediately, saying that for the first time they felt like a separate entity from the Giants.

You can also instill pride by praising things someone does that, perhaps, that person hasn't considered special. A man walks his wife to her car or cooks dinner for her one night. He doesn't think those are big deals, but to his wife, they are. If she doesn't let him know that, though, they become routine and dull. It's so easy to for her to say how much she appreciates those gestures, and knowing that she notices the "little things" he does as well as the big makes him proud of the way he approaches his relationship with her. Pride in a relationship is easy to obtain when you pay attention to actions and reactions. It's when you forget to pay that attention that a relationship becomes dull and stagnant.

In business, you need to praise the mail boy for bringing your mail promptly. Do that and you make him proud of something he might have taken for granted. Praise your boss for giving you a heads-up on an important company change, and he takes pride in knowing that he helped you prepare for something that affects your work. Praise your child's effort in getting a tough school project done early, and that becomes something he's proud of and most likely will continue to take pride in.

When I first got the job with the Jets, I searched and searched to find out what the NFL shield represented—you know, the crest that surrounds the letters NFL. I actually called the league, and I said, "Do you know what the shield stands for? Do you guys have a definition of the shield?" They went, "Well, no." I said, "Don't worry about it because I'm going to write what it stands for."

I told them that the red, white, and blue stands for the United States flag. And that the NFL was part of the fabric of American society and it was their responsibility to respect that shield as they do the flag.

As a rookie, I used to walk up the hill every day after practice with Roman Gabriel. He'd tell me stories; he'd tell me about the history of the league, how he prepared himself, what it took to succeed in the NFL. I was a rookie free agent listening to Roman Gabriel and getting all this for free. I've tried to pass it on. We have an obligation. The players need to know what that shield stands for. It's not a right, but a privilege to play in the NFL.

Autograph Your Performance

Make sure that whatever it is you do, you do it in a way that would make you proud to sign your name to it, like an artist signs a painting. I tell my players that means everything: how you act in public and in private, as well as on the football field.

To be a winner, you've got to act like a winner at all times: the way you carry yourself; the way you deal with your teammates, your coaches, people you know, and people you don't know. You never want to walk away from someone and have that person then say to someone else, "What a jerk."

Too many times I hear about people being cruel to someone they consider "beneath" them. They yell at the bellman; they curse the lady in the business center or the waitress who brings them the wrong order. To me, there is really no excuse for that type of behavior. People should be treated with respect, as long as they are doing the same for you. Belittling someone is not turning in a performance worth autographing—in fact, it's something that, when looked at from a distance, you really don't want to be associated with at all.

The same goes for showboating on the football field. I don't believe in using all these wild celebrations to autograph a performance. I like the spontaneous joy that comes from scoring a touchdown or making a big sack, but make sure that how you autograph what you just did doesn't put you into a category you don't want to be in.

Don't gloat, either. Say you've just finished a big project and the boss is very, very pleased and you're thrilled with what you've done. Don't walk around the office with your chest puffed out or start lighting cigars. Autograph that project with class. Thank those who helped you and then go back to what you were doing to get there in the first place.

People who gloat and brag, to me, are the most insecure people you can find. They feel the need to tell everyone who will listen, and even those who won't, about what they've done, or about what their kid has done, in a way that is almost offensive to those who do hear what that person has to say.

I heard about the father of a runner who had just gotten a scholarship to college. He was excited about his son's achievement, and rightly so, but he was so excited that he became insensitive to what other people were feeling. All day long at the meet, he kept walking up to other parents and saying, "Sam got a full ride to UT; isn't that great?" They'd reply politely, "Yes, congratulations, that's wonderful." And then he'd follow with, "Where's your son going?" Now, he may genuinely have wanted to know and not meant any harm, but suddenly the parent whose son hadn't gotten a college offer was put in a bad spot. And the guy never got it. All day long he went through the motions—bragging, boasting, and then putting people down. He was not autographing anything then; he was just alienating people.

I know that people by nature do things and say things they later regret. Sometimes it's an honest mistake. Sometimes it's simply reacting wrong and not paying attention to how what you say or do affects someone around you. The best advice I can give is to see yourself in the best light possible, where everyone says good things about you and no one says bad things behind your back. Visualize that, and then think about it before you say or do something, whether it be in the heat of anger or because of alcohol or whatever excuse you come up with for why that action is, in your mind, justified.

Many people have lost their jobs, lost their image, or lost their reputation because of a few bad judgments that affected their performance on a certain night or a certain day. Remember, you only have one reputation, one image; changing either is extremely difficult. I deal with reality, not perception. Make sure you're living a life that reflects what you stand for in the workplace, socially, at home with your kids, wherever you go. Because at the end of the day what you stood for tells the story of your life.

2001 NFL Coaches Questionnaire

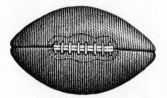

Name: Herman Lee Edwards.

Hobbies: Exercising and golfing.

Last Book Read (and Author): Run to Daylight by Vince Lombardi.

Favorite Food: BBQ chicken.

Favorite Vacation Spot: Hawaii.

Best Football Nickname: Billy "White Shoes" Johnson.

Favorite College Town: South Bend, Indiana.

Which NFL Team Did You Follow as a Child: The Dallas Cowboys.

Favorite Athlete as a Child: Muhammad Ali.

Favorite Stadium Other than Your Own and Why: Green Bay's Lambeau Field because of the rich tradition.

Favorite Sports Uniform Other than Your Own: The "old" Washington Redskins uniforms.

Favorite Other Sport: Golf.

Person You'd Most Like to Meet: I would have really liked to have met Mother Teresa.

Person Who Influenced You the Most: My parents, Herman Sr. and Martha Edwards.

Best Advice Ever Received: Be humble.

Player (Former or Current) Who'd Make a Great Head Coach: Tampa Bay safety John Lynch.

Greatest Overachiever You've Ever Coached: Kevin Ross (former Kansas City Chief).

Best Pure Athlete You've Ever Coached: Dale Carter.

Toughest Player You've Ever Coached: John Lynch.

Most Inspirational Player You've Ever Coached: Charles Dimry in Tampa Bay. His wife was sick with bone cancer, and he was raising their three young daughters, running the house, and playing football at a high level. I was amazed and inspired by him.

Funniest Player You've Ever Coached: Tampa Bay safety Dexter Jackson.

Toughest Coach You've Ever Faced: Tom Landry.

Greatest Team You've Ever Competed Against: The Dallas Cowboys and Pittsburgh Steelers teams of the 1970s.

Toughest Game You've Ever Competed in, as a Coach or Player: The Eagles vs. NY Giants at the Vet on 12/11/77, a PHI 17–14 win. It was such a physical game. I'll never forget it.

Loudest Crowd of Your Football Career, Home or Away: NFC Championship game at St. Louis in 1999 season (2000 postseason).

Most Knowledgeable Football Writer You've Ever Met: Ray Didenger, formerly of the *Philadelphia Daily News*.

Most Overrated Aspect of Football: Time of possession.

Most Underrated Aspect of Football: The power of teamwork and chemistry. It was evident with this year's Super Bowl teams. There was a strong cohesion among the players, and both teams embraced the team concept.

Who Has the Hardest Job in Football: The officials. They never have a home game.

Most Embarrassing Football Moment: I stumbled during player introductions when I was playing for the Eagles.

Most Memorable Football Moment: Playing in Super Bowl XV.

One Thing You'd Change About Pro Football: I think it should be mandatory that both teams be present for the singing of the national anthem. This is a great country we live in, and we should pay proper respect for the freedoms that we have.

One Thing That Should Never Change About Pro Football: I think that the most interesting thing about football is how people are fascinated with the size, speed, and strength elements of the players, but what really separates the players is those with the biggest hearts.

If You Weren't Coaching, What Would You Be Doing: I would be a teacher. I enjoy being around children and instructing.

Index

Index

Index

Index

Index

About the Authors

Herman Edwards is the head coach of the New York Jets. The only Jets coach to take his team to the playoffs in his first two seasons at the helm, Edwards in 2002 also became the first NFL coach since the 1970 merger to rally his team to the division title after a 2-5 start. The former standout defensive back for the Philadelphia Eagles has been a driving force in community projects wherever he has landed, including the Focus and Finish youth enrichment program he implemented while coaching with the Tampa Bay Buccaneers and the Herman Edwards Football Camp for underprivileged children in California's Monterey Peninsula.

Shelley Smith is an award-winning ESPN journalist. Smith also spent eight years as a writer and reporter for *Sport Illustrated*.